A BOOK OF
RAILWAY LOCOMOTIVES
FOR BOYS OF ALL AGES

"NORTH STAR"—— AS REBUILT IN 1854. CONSTRUCTED BY R. STEPHENSON & Co IN 1837.
"LORD OF THE ISLES"—— BUILT BY G. W. R. Co AT SWINDON IN 1851.
"CAERPHILLY CASTLE"—— DO. DO. DO. DO. DO. 1923.

ENGINE	CYLINDERS		DRIVING WHEELS	BOILER PRESSURE	TRACTIVE EFFORT AT 85% BOILER PRESSURE
	Nº	DIMENSIONS			
NORTH STAR.	2	16" x 18"	7' – 0"	80 LBS.°	3730 LBS.
LORD OF THE ISLES.	2	18" x 24"	8' – 0"	140 "	9640 "
CAERPHILLY CASTLE.	4	16" x 26"	6' – 8½"	225 "	31625 "

G.W.R. LOCOMOTIVES, 1838—1923. REPRODUCED TO THE SAME SCALE

"Caerphilly Castle"

A BOOK OF RAILWAY LOCOMOTIVES

FOR BOYS OF ALL AGES

BY W. G. CHAPMAN

(*Author of* "*The* 10.30 *Limited*")

PUBLISHED IN 1924 BY

THE GREAT WESTERN RAILWAY

[FELIX J. C. POLE, GENERAL MANAGER]

PADDINGTON STATION, LONDON

First published 1924
Reprinted 1970

ISBN 0 85059 057 4

Reproduced by offset lithography from the original by Reda SA, of Geneva, Switzerland, and bound by Hunter & Foulis Ltd, of Edinburgh, Scotland, for the publishers Patrick Stephens Limited, 9 Ely Place, London EC1, England

INTRODUCTION TO NEW EDITION

THE SECOND of W. G. Chapman's railway books for "Boys of All Ages" was written to fulfil the demand made apparent by the first book in the series, "The 10.30 Limited", which was published in 1923 and which has now also been reprinted by Patrick Stephens. In 1923 the "Castle" Class had only just appeared and brief mention of the fact was made in the earlier book. By 1924, 4073 "Caerphilly Castle"—the first of the Castle Class—was on show at the Wembley Exhibition and hailed to the world as the most powerful passenger train engine in the kingdom.

The chapter on speed enables the author to publicise several of the G.W.R.'s then current achievements, although by today's standards they are, of course, modest. For example, the book takes us on a visit to Swindon Works and "we really must make a point of timing our tour so as to return to London by the 3.45 p.m. from Swindon", which is described earlier as the fastest train in the British Empire and possibly the fastest start-to-stop run in the world at an average speed of 61.8 m.p.h.!

Other absorbing chapters include "The Engine Shed" which, amongst other things, gives the standard mileage figures and time intervals for periodical examination, and "The Engine Crew" and "Locomotive Running Tests" which give details of how tests were conducted on 4074 "Caldicot Castle" between Swindon and Plymouth. It is interesting to see that the photographs used to illustrate the chapter on "Erecting a Locomotive" show a build-up of 3137, a 2-6-2T, which is a surprisingly humble locomotive to portray in a prestige book such as this.

The book is brought to an enthusiastic conclusion with an account of a footplate run on that fastest train—still to be christened by the name "Cheltenham Flyer" which was bestowed on a later edition of the author's works that we also hope to re-issue in time. "Go Great Western" the book concludes. I, for one, only wish that it were still possible.

Norman Simmons

FOREWORD

SOME years ago, so the story goes, there stood on the platform at Paddington Station a father and his small son, the latter armed with a bag of buns obtained from the adjacent Refreshment Rooms. These two were watching the departure of a train. " What *makes* the engine go ? " asked young hopeful of the fount of all knowledge. " Ah," responded the fond parent, " it's like this. You see there is the steam in the boiler, and the—er—boiler, that is, of course, there's the boiler and the steam and—er—oh, *bother the engine*, eat your buns."

Verily, no man knows how little he knows until his children begin to ask him questions.

This happened, as already stated, some years ago, long before the year of grace 1923, which was marked by the appearance of a little book entitled " The 10.30 Limited " —" A Railway Book for Boys of all Ages," which essayed to explain for the edification and enlightenment of just such small boys and just such fond parents some of the " hows," " whys," and " wherefores " of modern railway practice.

It is regretted that in some accounts of the incident referred to there is a monosyllabic substitution for the word " bother " which can only be condemned. Whatever may be the authentic version, however, there is consensus of opinion in support of the statement that the child's thirst for knowledge went unquenched even if his appetite for buns was appeased.

Any temptation to dilate upon the excellent qualities

of the buns supplied at Great Western Railway Refreshment Rooms is resisted. The incident is only recalled for the reason that it confirms an impression, formed from many letters received from readers of " The 10.30 Limited," that there is a demand for more information with regard to the railway locomotive. Whilst all phases of railway operation appear to be of absorbing interest to " boys of all ages," the locomotive is doubtless the *pièce de résistance.*

In " The 10.30 Limited " an attempt was made to afford general information with regard to some aspects of railway working, but it was obviously impossible to deal at any length with such a subject as the railway locomotive, particularly as the whole narrative was contained within the few short hours occupied by the run of the " wonder train to the west." Among a wealth of literature upon the subject of railways there is still room for a book which will explain to the young reader in more detail the story of the " greyhound of the iron track."

These must be the excuses, if any are needed, for this little volume " Caerphilly Castle."

The title has been selected for the reason that the super-locomotive so named, and recently produced at the Great Western Railway Company's Works at Swindon, constitutes the last word in railway locomotive construction, and is, in fact, the most powerful passenger train engine in the Kingdom.

The reader is to assume that the following pages record the resumption of a chat by the author with his youthful companion of " The 10.30 Limited."

W.G.C.

READING, JULY 1924

CHAPTERS

WITH 155 ILLUSTRATIONS

CHAPTER THE FIRST

EARLY DAYS

I AM not at all surprised that after our chat upon railway working on the occasion of our recent trip by "The 10.30 Limited" you still want to know more about the engines. Since the earliest days of railways, the locomotives have not ceased to fascinate succeeding generations of boys, young and old, for they seem to have a magnetic charm which is peculiarly their own.

The story of the advent of the railway locomotive has been told so many times and in so many ways that I do not propose to weary you with a reiteration of it to-day, but rather lightly to touch on the earliest days of railways, and then to trace the evolution of the locomotive on the Great Western Railway, stage by stage, from the earliest types to the giant engines of to-day.

We will try and steer clear of all technicalities, but if, here and there, a word or phrase should occur, the meaning of which is not quite clear, our subsequent chat on the various parts of the locomotive, their respective functions and relation to one another will, I think, disperse any doubts or difficulties in your mind.

When we have followed the evolution of the locomotive from " North Star " to " Caerphilly Castle," and discussed the various types of engines and their uses, we are going to make a short tour of the Great Western Railway Locomotive Works at Swindon, where we shall see engines in the various stages of construction, and the different parts of the engines in course of manufacture.

Although the name of George Stephenson is more often associated than any other with the introduction of the rail-

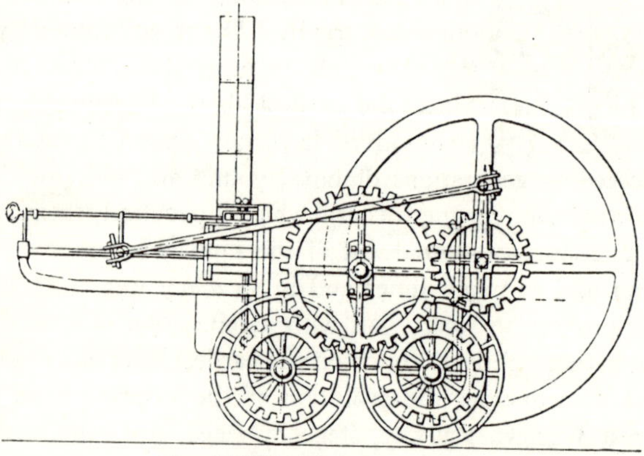

Trevithick's First Locomotive

way locomotive, it is not correct to say that Stephenson was its inventor, as at least one encyclopædia does, and as one of our leading daily newspapers did quite recently. There is little doubt that in the closing years of the eighteenth and early part of the nineteenth centuries many clever men contributed valuable ideas towards the solution of the problem of steam haulage of vehicles on railways. Richard Trevithick is said to have built the first railway locomotive in 1802, and his second was employed in hauling coal wagons on the Merthyr Tydvil tramroad in 1804. It is recorded that, as the result of a wager, this second engine, which is said to have "travelled with ease at five miles an hour," won its backer a bet of five hundred guineas. In the following decade several locomotives, which were more or less successful, were built for colliery work.

Richard Trevithick

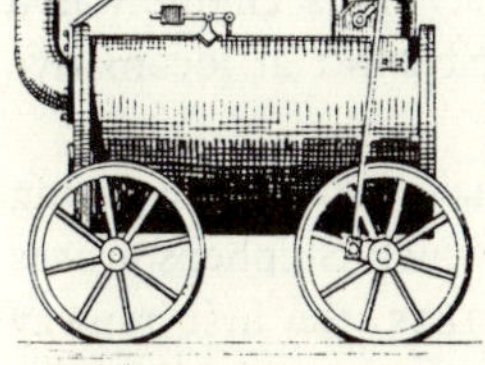

Trevithick's 1804 Locomotive

George Stephenson was born in 1781 at Wylam, Newcastle-on-Tyne, where his father was employed as fireman for the Wylam Colliery pumping engine. George Stephenson never went to a day school, and it is said that at eighteen years of age he had not learnt to read. When fourteen years old he was assisting his father in firing the Wylam engine at a wage of 1*s.* a day. Three years later, when a new pit was opened in connection with the Wylam Colliery, Stephenson was appointed engineman, his father acting as fireman for him. It is said that young George extended his knowledge of the steam-engine by taking his charge to pieces during holidays and week-ends.

Stephenson's first locomotive, "Blucher," constructed for the Killingworth Colliery, was tried in July 1814. It is quite evident that on this and subsequent engines Stephenson embodied and improved upon features of previous locomotives and added ideas of his own.

George Stephenson

The engine "Blucher" had spur gearing—that is, the pistons were connected with spur (cog) wheels which engaged with cogs on the four driving wheels. This engine was not altogether successful, and in 1815 Stephenson built his second locomotive, in which the pistons were connected by cross-bars and connecting rods directly to the driving wheels. This engine was a considerable improvement on his first effort at locomotive construction.

Further improvements appear to have taken place during the next ten years, with many of which Stephenson was associated, and on September 25, 1825, the first railway (Stockton and Darlington) was opened to the public. On this historic occasion Stephenson, who had been appointed Engineer to the Railway Company, was the driver of his engine "Locomotion," which hauled a train of thirty-four vehicles behind the tender. The load was a mixed one, consisting of six wagons filled with merchandise and coal, a covered passenger vehicle for the railway directors and their friends, twenty-one open wagons fitted with seats for passengers, and, lastly, six wagons loaded with coal. Presumably the wagons were small coal trucks of about three to four tons' capacity as used for horse haulage on the railroad. It is rather strange to read that a man on horseback rode in front of the engine to clear the line!

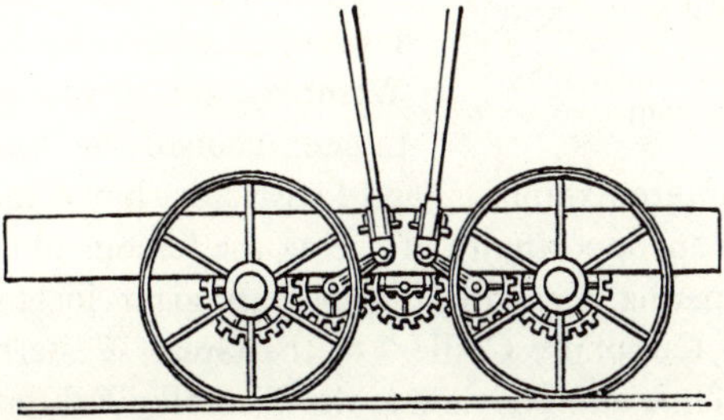

Driving Gear of Stephenson's First Locomotive, 1814

It was on Stephenson's advice that the directors of the Stockton and Darlington Railway applied for and obtained parliamentary powers to use steam, and there appears little doubt that, to quote Green's "Short History of the English People," his "belief in the potentialities of steam made staid and unreceptive people think he was beside himself." This epoch-making event seems, however, to have had little more than local interest at the time, for the "Annual Register," which essayed to contain a review of events and a retrospect of scientific progress, made no mention of the opening at all. It is doubtful, however, if any change introduced in the whole of the nineteenth century was to have greater effect upon the lives of the people.

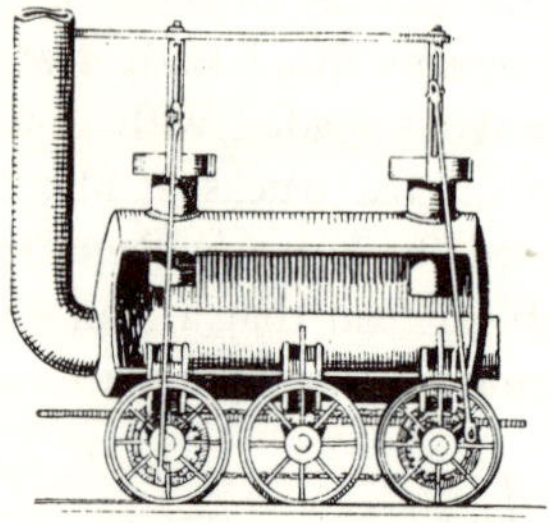

Stephenson's 1815 Locomotive

Although the first railway was opened nearly a century ago, old "Locomotion" still survives, and for many years stood on the platform at Darlington Bank Top Railway Station. She has recently, however, been conveyed to Wembley, and if you are fortunate enough to visit the British Empire Exhibition (and I wish *every* boy could), you will have an opportunity of seeing the famous old engine and comparing her with the modern giant locomotives, such as "Caerphilly Castle" of the Great Western Railway, which is also on view at the Wembley Exhibition.

Stephenson's "Locomotion"

"Locomotion" had four coupled wheels. There was one large flue or tube through the boiler, the cylinders being placed vertically and half within the boiler. The exhaust steam from the cylinders was discharged into the chimney. The boiler, worked at a pressure of 52 lb. per sq. in., is 10 ft. long by 4 ft.

diameter, and has 60 sq. ft. of heating surface. The two vertical cylinders were originally 9 in. diameter and the stroke 24 in., the piston rods being guided by parallel motions by means of a crosshead and bar and connecting rods. The wheels are 4 ft. diameter and the weight of the engine, without coal or water, is 6 tons 16 cwt.

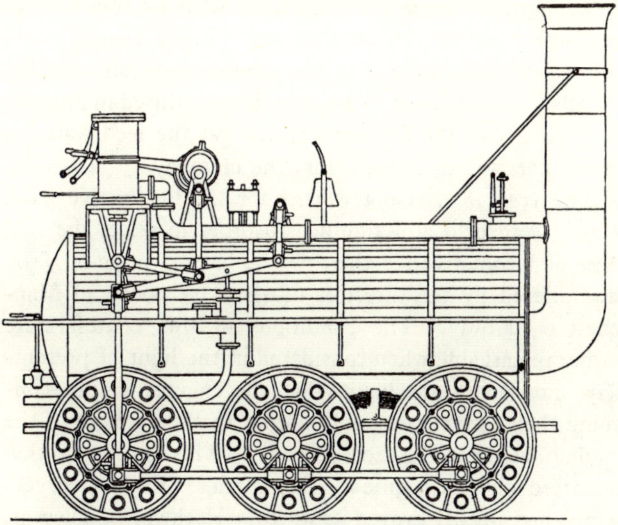

Hackworth's " Royal George "

Stephenson established locomotive works at Newcastle, where his only son Robert and a clever manager, Timothy Hackworth (whose influence on the development of the locomotive has, perhaps, not been fully recognised), were associated in the production of " Locomotion."

In 1827 Hackworth produced for the Stockton and Darlington Railway a famous engine, " Royal George," which embodied several important improvements in locomotive construction. This engine deserves more than passing notice, for, when it appeared, the fate of the locomotive was still in the balance, and there was a possibility of returning to horse haulage on the Stockton and Darlington Railway. Before definitely coming to a decision, it was agreed to let Hackworth see what he could do to produce a reliable locomotive, and "Royal George" was the result. She was the first engine with six coupled wheels. The exhaust steam, which was utilised to increase the draught of the furnace and to heat the feed water to the boiler, was discharged into the chimney

The year 1829 is noteworthy for the locomotive trials which were held at Rainhill. In order to select the best type of locomotive for their new railway, a prize of £500 was offered by the directors of the Liverpool and Manchester Railway. The conditions of this contest were rather remarkable when considered in the light of present-day knowledge, one being that the engines should consume their own smoke, and another that the weight of the engine should not exceed six tons! This latter condition debarred such an engine as Hackworth's "Royal George," which had already proved its worth. Hackworth, however, built and entered a new locomotive—"Sanspareil"—which, unfortunately, burst a cylinder when on trial. Another promising entry—"Novelty"—developed boiler troubles, and, as you probably know, Robert Stephenson's famous "Rocket" won the contest. She averaged thirteen and a half miles an hour during her trial, and reached a maximum speed of twenty-four miles an hour.

"Rocket" was the first railway locomotive fitted with

tubes for increasing the heating surface of the boiler. There were twenty-five copper tubes of 3 in. diameter fitted in the cylindrical boiler, which was 6 ft. in length. The front wheels of the engine were driven directly from the cylinders by means of connecting rods attached to the pistons. Engine and tender in working order weighed $4\frac{1}{4}$ tons. "Rocket" is now in the South Kensington

"Rocket"

Museum, where she rests from her labours alongside her competitor "Sanspareil." The latter, though beaten in the Rainhill trials, did good work for many years.

The Rainhill trials may be regarded as having, to a large extent, settled the future of the steam locomotive. They also did much to make the name of Robert Stephenson famous in connection with locomotives and railways.

Perhaps you are not aware that Robert Stephenson was the godfather of a man admired by boys the world over.

I refer to Sir Robert Baden Powell, the Chief Scout and founder of the Boy Scout Movement, now world-wide. Sir Robert's full names are Robert Stephenson Smyth Baden Powell.

The Liverpool and Manchester Railway, the first railway of any magnitude, was opened in 1830, and George Stephenson was again selected as Engineer. He was on the footplate of "Northumbrian" at the opening ceremony, when among the distinguished spectators was the Duke of Wellington.

From this time onwards many railways were projected and constructed, and, in 1838, the first portion of the Great Western Railway, built by the famous engineer Isambard Kingdom Brunel, was opened to the public. In the intervening years the railway locomotive had been considerably developed and improved by a number of builders, but, so far, none of the railway companies had established its own locomotive works.

CHAPTER THE SECOND

OLD BROAD GAUGERS

THE first locomotives acquired by the Great Western Railway Company and used at the opening of the line from London to Maidenhead on June 4, 1838, caused the youthful locomotive superintendent, Mr. Daniel Gooch, such continuous trouble and anxiety that he soon started designing engines to his own ideas. Mr. Gooch (afterwards Sir Daniel Gooch, and Chairman of the Great Western Railway Company) had been appointed Locomotive Superintendent when only twenty-one years of age by Brunel, who, by the way, was only twenty-seven years old when he took up his duties as Engineer to the Company in 1833. This appears to have been an age of great opportunities and of clever young men ready to seize them.

Sir Daniel Gooch

The following extract from Mr. Gooch's diary tells the

story of his appointment to the position which he held for upwards of a quarter of a century. It also describes the commencement of the locomotive history of the Great Western Railway Company, and affords some idea of the troubles and trials of those early days :

Towards the end of July, 1837, I heard that Mr. Brunel wanted someone to take the post of locomotive engineer on the Great Western Railway, and I at once went to him, on July 20th, preferring that department to railway making. . . . I heard from Mr. Brunel on the 2nd August saying he was coming into the North, and that he would call and see me. This gave me brighter hopes, and he called at the office on the 9th August, and arranged I should go to him at once. . . . I left Manchester and went to London, beginning my duties with the Great Western on the 18th August.

. . . None of the engines had then been delivered, although several were ordered. My first work was to prepare plans for the engine-houses at Paddington and Maidenhead, and I then went to inspect the engines then building. I was not much pleased with the design of the engines ordered. They had very small boilers and cylinders, and very large wheels. Those made by the Vulcan Company had wheels 8 ft. in diameter, and three of them only 12 in. cylinders with 18 in. stroke; two of Mather Dixon's had 10 ft. wheels and 14 in. cylinders, with very small boilers. Those made by Hawthorne were on a patent plan of Tom Harrison's, having the engine and boiler on separate carriages, and coupled with ball-and-socket steam pipes.

These were immense affairs; the boilers were very large, and cylinders were, I think, 16 in. diameter, and about 2 ft. stroke. In one, the cylinders were coupled direct to the driving wheels, which were 10 ft. diameter, and the other had a spur and pinion 3 to 1, with 6 ft. wheel, making the wheel equal to 18 ft. diameter. The same plan of gearing was used in the two engines built by the Haigh Foundry; their wheels were 6 ft.

diameter and the gearing 2 to 1, but the cylinders were small. I felt very uneasy about the working of these machines, feeling sure they would have enough to do to drive themselves along the road.

The first engine delivered to the railway was the "Vulcan," built by the Vulcan Foundry Company. She was first in steam on the rail on the 9th January, 1838; a second from the same firm, and two from Mather Dixon & Co., followed in a week or so. These came by canal to West Drayton, and I had to get them from there to the engine-house, about a mile off. The "North Star" engine was delivered by barge on the river at Maidenhead in January, 1838. The first running of the engines was celebrated by a dinner at West Drayton on the 18th January.

I was much engaged up to the end of May in getting all ready for opening the portion of the Great Western Railway from London to Maidenhead. On the 31st May, 1838, the directors made their first trip over the whole length of this portion, and it was opened to the public on the 4th June, and then my difficulties with the engines began. The "North Star" and the six from the Vulcan Foundry Company were the only ones I could at all depend upon. For many weeks my nights were spent in a carriage in the engine-house at Paddington, as repairs had to be done to the engines at night to get them to do their work next day. The "North Star," being the most powerful one and in other respects the best, was my chief reliance, but she was often getting into trouble from other causes.

"North Star" was one of the first, and certainly appears to have been the most successful, of the engines supplied to the Great Western Railway at that time. It was built by Robert Stephenson & Co., in 1837, and its name was evidently a favourite one with the makers, who had built their first "North Star" for the Liverpool and Manchester Railway in 1830. The "North Star" of the Great Western Railway was of Robert Stephenson's standard design of the period at which it was built, except for the diameter of the driving wheels, which were of the then unusual size of 7 ft., adopted by Stephenson in this case to meet Brunel's wish for higher speeds than had hitherto prevailed.

This engine and the "Morning Star" were originally intended for the New Orleans Railway, with a gauge of 5 ft. 6 in., but—to quote Robert Stephenson's own words before the Gauge Commission, 1845—"in consequence of the panic that came over the commercial world"

"North Star"

they were not sent out to America, but lay on his hands until, after the necessary alteration, they had been adapted to the 7 ft. gauge of the Great Western Railway, and the driving wheels of one of them made specially large.

You will notice that Mr. Gooch regarded "North Star" as the most powerful and reliable of these early engines. As originally built by Robert Stephenson and Co., it had cylinders 15 in. diameter by 18 in. stroke, and was fitted with what was known as "Gab" motion. The boiler had a dome on the barrel and two separate valves, one locked and one spring loaded on the barrel. About the year 1854, the boiler was lengthened some 5 inches, the dome removed entirely and the safety valves combined and placed together on the existing manhole on the fire-box. In this condition "Gooch" expansion gear was also fitted and the cylinders were enlarged. It worked until the year 1870 and covered a total mileage of 429,000. The principal dimensions were :

Cylinders	16 in. diameter × 18 in. stroke.	
Driving wheels	7 ft. ,,	
Leading and trailing wheels	4 ft. ,,	
Heating surface :		
Tubes	654·7 sq. ft.	Total, 724·8 sq. ft.
Fire-box	70·1 ,,	
Grate area	13·0 ,,	
Boiler pressure	100 lb. per sq. in.	

Mr. Gooch's diary continues :

The failure of so many engines made the directors very anxious, and they called upon me, apart from Mr. Brunel, to make them a report on each engine.

Mr. Gooch goes on to relate how he felt himself placed in great difficulty in having to report independently from his chief. He had no choice in the matter, however, and his report condemned the construction of the engines. This naturally alarmed the directors, and he was shortly afterwards instructed to prepare designs for additional locomotives, of which it had become necessary to order a large number. Mr. Gooch records that he took great pains with the drawings, and he produced designs for two classes of engines, one with a 7 ft. driving wheel, 15 in. cylinder, and 18 in. stroke, but with ample boiler power.

When Mr. Gooch had completed the drawings for the

new engines referred to, contracts were let for no fewer than 142 locomotives from various makers, the first to be delivered being the "Firefly" in 1840.

"Firefly"

In this year Swindon was decided upon as the site for the Locomotive, Carriage and Wagon Works of the Great Western Railway. In this connection, the following further quotation from Mr. Gooch's diary is interesting:

> 1840. During this year further portions of the Great Western were opened and agreements were made for leasing the Bristol and Exeter and the Swindon and Cheltenham Railways, and it became necessary to furnish large works for the repair, etc., of our stock. I was called upon to report on the best situation to build these works, and on full consideration I reported in favour of Swindon, it being the junction with the Cheltenham branch and also a convenient division of the Great Western line for the engine working. Mr. Brunel and I went to look at the ground, then only green fields, and he agreed with me as to its being the best place.

In a recent work on railways the author says that Brunel and Gooch were one day taking an *al fresco* lunch at the side of the new railway and discussing just where the locomotive works should be erected. They agreed to throw a stone, and where it fell a peg should be driven in the ground, which should mark the site for the Works.

Whether this story is true or not it is difficult to say at this date. Anyway, decisions of the kind are not made quite like that nowadays.

This photograph of Swindon, taken in 1847, shews "Firebrand," a sister engine to "Firefly." Swindon was quite a small place when the railway was constructed,

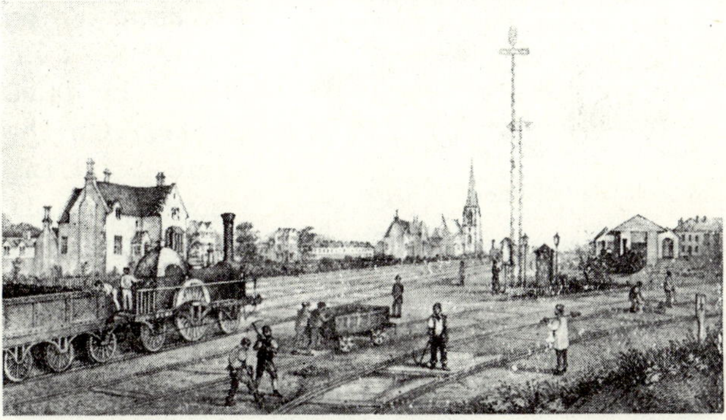

Swindon in 1847

but now it has a population of 57,000. By 1876 the number of employees at the Works had reached 4,500, and to-day the figure is about 14,000.

"Ixion," a similar engine to "North Star," was used by Mr. Gooch in 1845 in his experiments when preparing information for the Gauge Commission, appointed to inquire into and report upon the respective merits of the broad (7 ft.) gauge (to which the Great Western Railway was then constructed) and the narrow (4 ft. $8\frac{1}{2}$ in.) gauge. Mr. Gooch was a witness before the Commission on behalf of the broad gauge. Several trips were made between London and Didcot with a maximum load of 81 tons behind the tender, at a maximum speed of 59 miles per hour on a falling gradient—Didcot-London—1 in 1,070. For the trials with a goods train the engine "Sampson" was used. It had six coupled wheels of 5 ft. diameter, and cylinders 15 in. diameter by 18 in. stroke. On the same falling gradient the engine obtained an average speed of 25.7 miles per hour, with 400 tons behind the tender. Mr. Gooch stated that, in 1845, the express trains of the Great Western Railway were timed at an average over-all speed of 44 miles per hour, and a maximum speed of 60 miles per hour, between Twyford and Maidenhead, with loads of 70 or 80 tons behind the tender.

"Ixion"

In 1845 the line was being worked by the following engines:

No.	*Type*	*Diameter of Driving Wheels*	*Cylinders*	*Heating Surface*			*Fire-grate Area*
				Fire-box	*Tubes*	*Total*	
				sq. ft.	sq. ft.	sq. ft.	sq. ft.
72	2-2-2	7 ft.	15″ or 15½″ × 18″	97·0	602	699·0	13·5
30	2-2-2	6 ft.	14″ × 18″	88·7	519	607·7	12·5
22	2-4-0	5 ft.	15″ × 18″	71·0	396	467·0	11·4
4	0-6-0	5 ft.	15″ × 18″	—	—	—	—

In his evidence before the Gauge Commissioners, Mr. Gooch stated that he proposed to build engines of greater power, and in 1846 "Great Western," the first of the famous "eight-foot singles," was built at Swindon. It was originally of the 2–2–2 type, but the weight on the leading wheels was found to be too great, and an extra pair of wheels was added. The engine had a dome-top fire-box, but this form was abandoned on the succeeding engines

Longitudinal Section Gooch 8 ft. Single

in favour of the ordinary round-top fire-box. In the latter form (4–2–2) twenty-four engines were built at Swindon and seven by an outside builder. "Gooch" link motion was fitted, and the cylinders were 18 in. diameter by 24 in. stroke, the boiler pressure being 120 lb. A feature of these locomotives was that the tenders were provided with a seat at the back facing the train for the "travelling porter," whose duty it was to warn the driver if anything happened to the train. The exponents of the narrow gauge facetiously referred to this porter as "the man in the iron coffin," and alleged that he was placed in the tender to give notice of the many dangers to which travellers on the broad gauge were exposed!

It is doubtful if any locomotives have so famous a history as Gooch's old broad gauge engines. With their large single driving wheels, brass-mounted boilers and wheel covers, they were indeed examples of symmetrical beauty. The famous "Lord of the Isles," built in 1851,

" Lord of the Isles "

was probably the fastest and most powerful broad gauge locomotive ever constructed. She was in regular service for nearly thirty years, during which she ran 789,300 miles with her original boiler still intact. She was on view at the Great Exhibition of 1851, the Edinburgh Exhibition of 1890, the Chicago Exposition of 1893, and the Earl's Court Exhibition of 1897.

Wonderful stories are told of the achievements of these old broad gauge expresses. It is said that one of the drivers solemnly offered to attempt a run of $118\frac{1}{4}$ miles from London to Bristol in an hour, and thoroughly believed he could do it if permitted.

These engines were actually *booked* to leave Didcot (53 miles from Paddington) fifty-seven minutes after their departure time from London, and repeatedly did the run in fifty minutes, and often in less.

It is recorded that a broad gauge express train, hauled by one of Gooch's fliers, with a load of 100 tons, covered the 118¼ miles from London to Bristol in two hours twelve minutes, inclusive of nine and a half minutes spent in stoppages *en route*.

Between 1846 and 1864, when he was succeeded as Locomotive Superintendent by Mr. Joseph Armstrong, Mr. Gooch built at the Swindon Works upwards of 120 0–6–0 type broad gauge goods engines with 5 ft. wheels. The first twelve had cylinders 16 in. diameter by 24 in. stroke, but the remainder were given one extra inch in diameter, the stroke remaining the same. In addition sixteen of the " eight-footers " were built, and towards the latter part of this period ten " Metropolitan " side tanks were turned out, with four coupled wheels 6 ft. diameter and cylinders 16 in. diameter by 24 in. stroke. During this time also, as engines of the older types were brought in for repairs, efficiency was improved, principally by means of increased boiler and cylinder capacity.

You have already heard something of the " Battle of the Gauges," which was waged in the early days of railways between the advocates of the broad (7 ft.) gauge, as originally adopted by Brunel on the Great Western Railway, and the narrow (now standard) gauge (4 ft. 8½ in.), and we have referred once or twice to the Gauge Commission appointed to report upon the merits of the respective gauges. The Commissioners sat from August to December, 1845, examining forty-eight witnesses. Thirty-five were direct advocates of the narrow gauge, eight (all locomotive engineers) favoured a gauge of from 5 to 6 ft., and the remainder—which included Brunel, Gooch, and other Great Western officers—were broad gauge champions. At the close of the inquiry Brunel suggested that, to test the accuracy of the opinions which had been expressed, engine trials be made under the eyes of the Commissioners. The narrow gauge party, however, on various pleas refused to commit themselves to long distance running; it was therefore agreed that trials should be made with trainloads of sixty, seventy and eighty tons between London and Didcot, a distance of fifty-three miles, and between York and Darlington, about forty-five miles. The carrying out of the trials completed the evidence taken by the Commissioners and proved the undoubted superiority of broad gauge engines.

It is interesting to recall that the Gauge Commissioners, in their report of 1846, said:

> We feel it a duty to observe that the public are mainly indebted for the present rate of speed and the increased accommodation of railway carriages to the genius of Mr. Brunel and the liberality of the Great Western Railway Company.

This was a tribute to the genius of Gooch as well as to that of Brunel.

The report of the Commissioners, however, sounded the death knell of the ambitious broad gauge of which Brunel and Gooch were the active pioneers, although its doom was not complete until 1892.

Mr. Daniel Gooch became Chairman of the Great Western Railway in November 1865, and was created a baronet in the following year.

CHAPTER THE THIRD

BROAD TO STANDARD GAUGE

The narrow gauge having been approved by the Commission, an Act for regulating the gauge of railways was passed rendering it unlawful to construct new lines in Great Britain other than of 4 ft. 8½ in. gauge without express Parliamentary sanction. This made the ultimate standardisation of the narrow gauge inevitable, and a third rail was laid on a good deal of the broad gauge, so that it could be used by vehicles of either gauge.

With the advent of this " mixed gauge " and the amalgamation of other lines came the need for narrow gauge locomotives. The first of these was built at Swindon in 1855. Its official designation was " a six wheels coupled, double sandwich framed, goods tender engine." It comes as something of a relief to find that it was also numbered " 57." This engine was rebuilt in 1870 at the G.W.R. Works at Wolverhampton, and subsequently boiler renewals, etc., were effected. So well did this engine hold out that she was in active service until November 1912. During those fifty-seven years she ran 1,023,754 miles.

When Mr. Joseph Armstrong succeeded Mr. Gooch in

the position of Locomotive Superintendent in 1864, there was a demand for narrow gauge engines, to meet which Mr. Armstrong designed standard goods engines of the 0–6–0 class, Metropolitan passenger tank engines (i.e. 6 ft. coupled driving and trailing wheels), and some famous 7 ft. singles. The first of these, No. 378, built in 1866, he named "Sir Daniel," a compliment to his predecessor. This engine, with later productions of the same type, did the bulk of the narrow gauge express passenger work for many years. As originally constructed, they had 7 ft. driving wheels; cylinders 17 in. by 24 in. stroke; boiler 11 ft. long, 4 ft. 2 in. diameter.

Another famous engine of Mr. Armstrong's design was No. 439, of which type six were built. They had 6 ft. driving wheels, four wheels coupled (2–4–0), cylinders 16 in. by 24 in. stroke; boiler 10 ft. 6 in. long by 4 ft. diameter. This type is of particular interest, as it was the precursor of the "Barnums" designed by Mr. Dean (Mr. Armstrong's successor) and of later ones by Mr. Churchward (Mr. Dean's successor). Their present-day representatives are the famous "Cities," which have 18 in. by 26 in. cylinders.

In the last year of Mr. Armstrong's regime, 1876, the Bristol and Exeter, and South Devon and Cornwall Railways were absorbed by—or perhaps we ought, for the sake of our West country friends, to say amalgamated with—the Great Western. This added nearly two hundred broad gauge engines (principally tank) to the Great Western stock. Some of the old Bristol and Exeter tank engines had immense (8 ft. 10 in.) driving wheels and a bogie at each end. You will probably be surprised to hear that these large driving wheels, which were nearly level with the top of the boiler, were flangeless. The weight on each of the bogies was 15 tons 12 cwt., and on the driving wheels 18 tons. One thousand gallons of water were carried in the back tank and four hundred gallons in a tank between the frames.

These engines were built by Messrs. Rothwell and Company in 1868 to designs of Mr. Pearson of the Bristol and Exeter Railway. They were fitted with hand brakes operating on the trailing bogies only. When taken over by the Great Western Railway they were altered to broad gauge tender engines, the trailing bogie was taken away and a pair of 4 ft. 6 in. trailing wheels substituted, thus converting them into 4–2–2's. They continued in service till 1890.

Mention should be made of the South Devon engines. They were tank engines, named, but not numbered, and principally built by the Avonside Company, Bristol, although a few had originally been purchased from the Great Western Railway. The engine illustrated on p. 26 (afterwards numbered 2132) had four 5 ft. 6 in. coupled wheels (4–4–0). The goods engines were six coupled tanks with 4 ft. 6 in. driving wheels (0–6–0). The majority of the South Devon engines continued to run until the alteration of the gauge in 1892.

Mr. William Dean succeeded Mr. Armstrong as Locomotive Superintendent in 1877, and between that year and 1889 he added considerably to the stock of standard goods and passenger engines, particularly the former, a large number of which were necessary owing to the amazing increase in mineral and goods traffic on the railway.

In 1889 he produced twenty narrow gauge 2–4–0 class engines, with 6 ft. 2 in. driving wheels; and in 1892 twenty to the same design, but with 6 ft. 8½ in. driving wheels. Two years later appeared the first of the single wheel engines, with 7 ft. 8½ in. driving wheels, which were regarded as successors to the famous broad gauge "eight-footers." Eight were built in this year, 2–2–2 type, broad gauge, but designed to be easily convertible to narrow gauge. This was done in 1892, and two others were subsequently built.

South Devon Broad Gauge Tank Engine

Afterwards a bogie was substituted for a single pair of leading wheels. Thirty of these were built in 1894, and twenty in 1897. These engines have done excellent work with light loads, but not being suitable for present day heavy traffic, being short of adhesion, have gradually been broken up as the need for heavier engines arose.

On Saturday and Sunday, the 21st and 22nd May, 1892, the broad gauge was finally abolished. Preparations for the change had been taking place for many years previously by building engines that were "convertible."

Broad Gauge Convertible Engine

At the date of the conversion the broad gauge engine stock consisted of 197, of which 130 were convertible.

In 1895 Mr. Dean built the first engine of 4-4-0 type with 5 ft. 8 in. driving wheels, for working over the heavy in-

Broad Gauge Conversion Stock at Swindon

clines in the west country, and so successful was this engine that forty of the type (" Devonshires ") were built in 1895 and 1896. In the latter year the first 4–6–0 type engine, with 4 ft. 7½ in. driving wheels, and cylinders 24 in. diameter by 20 in. stroke, was built for heavy goods work, and in 1899 a modification of this design produced the "Krugers." These had 4 ft. 7½ in. driving wheels, and cylinders 19 in. diameter by 28 in. stroke, fitted with piston valves. The following year witnessed the production of the "Badmintons," the forerunners of the "Cities."

Before continuing the history of Great Western Railway locomotives we might, I think, at this juncture, refer with

4-4-0 "Duke of Cornwall"

advantage to some of the changes introduced which had a marked effect upon the development of both the construction and working of the locomotive. Before doing so, however, and as we shall refer to developments beyond the point where we left our history, I ought to state that Mr. Dean was succeeded in 1902 by Mr. Churchward. During the latter's regime of nineteen years, the title of Locomotive Superintendent was changed to that of Chief Mechanical Engineer.

The outstanding items then were (*a*) the introduction and improvement of the automatic vacuum brake, 1876–1883; (*b*) the increase in the working pressure of boilers—

viz. from 75 lb. to 120 lb. per sq. in. in Mr. Gooch's time; from 120 lb. to 160 lb. per sq. in. in Mr. Armstrong's time; from 160 lb. to 180 lb. in Mr. Dean's time; reaching as high as 225 lb. in Mr. Churchward's time; (*c*) the provision of water-troughs, which have helped so materially in long distance non-stop passenger and goods train runs; (*d*) the introduction of water-softening plants, resulting in appreciably reducing the attention necessary to boilers at running depots; (*e*) superheating; and (*f*) top-feed to boilers (Mr. Churchward).

These continued efforts of successive Locomotive Superintendents made the G.W.R. locomotive a machine of remarkable utility and dependability.

Last Broad Gauge Train to the West in Sonning Cutting, May 20th, 1892

CHAPTER THE FOURTH

STANDARDISATION

We hear so much in these latter days of the advantages of standardisation and mass production of motor-cars and such-like, that one might imagine that standardisation in industry was some new departure. Its advantages have been very fully realised in regard to the construction and maintenance of locomotives on the Great Western Railway for many years past.

You have doubtless frequently heard the name of Henry Ford, the American motor-car manufacturer, associated with standardisation in industry. You may not know, however, that Mr. Ford started his career as an apprentice in the machine shop of an engine works in the United States. Possibly—I use the word guardedly—he was *there* impressed with the value of standardisation.

The term " standardisation of locomotives " does not, as is sometimes supposed, refer to the types of locomotives merely, but also to the parts thereof, such as boilers, bogies, cylinders, motion, expansion gear, etc., so as to render them interchangeable for various types of engines.

Between 1898 and 1900 the fleet of " Devonshires " was augmented. The last twenty—known as " Bulldogs " on account of the impression of massive strength they gave as compared with other engines at that time—were fitted with the standard No. 2 boiler. In 1900 and 1901 the "Atbaras," a further development of the "Badmintons," were turned out; these being somewhat similar to the "Bulldogs."

In August 1900 the first of the "Aberdares," 2–6–0 class (No. 33), was built. This class was a successor to the "Krugers." The following year more of these were built to the same drawings, and since that time the number has been further increased, but the engines have been fitted with larger boilers.

In 1903 the Company purchased from France a "de Glehn" compound locomotive (4–4–2) and in 1905 two more of greater power. Although these are not Great Western standard, they have been brought within the "interchangeability-of-boiler" scheme, and now carry standard boilers.

I should here mention that early in 1904, the first

Rail Motor Car and Trailer

rail motor car was built at Swindon. The Great Western Railway now has fifty-three of these cars, some of which are 70 feet in length. They have the same sized engines and boilers which are interchangeable throughout. The cars can be used with or without trailers, and, when engaged in a " shuttle " service, can be driven from the engine end or from the other end of the trailer, as desired.

In 1907 the increasing need for an engine for long non-stop runs (as, for instance, the Cornish Riviera and Fishguard Boat services) became pressing, and the first Great Western " four-cylinder "—No. 40 (now 4,000)—was constructed. It was built experimentally with a 4–4–2 wheel arrangement, but later was altered to the 4–6–0 type, a great many of which are now in service.

In June 1908 the first engine of the " Pacific " type (4-6-2), built in this country, viz. No. 111, " The Great Bear," was completed. In December 1910 the first engines of the 2-8-0T type were built, and in June 1911 the first of the 2-6-0 outside cylinder engines was produced.

It must not be forgotten that the provision of greater power in a locomotive means also increased weight, and until the permanent way, on what may be termed the subsidiary portions of the railway, is strengthened, it will be necessary to continue the use of some of the older designs of lighter and less powerful locomotives.

And now you have, I think, the locomotive history of the Great Western Railway up to about the war period. From 1914 onwards a number of standard engines was added to stock. As the war went on, however, and the necessity for increasing the output of munitions became a matter of vital urgency, more and more war work was undertaken at Swindon. We shall have something more to say about this on our visit there.

In 1919 the 4700 class, a new type of 2–8–0 engine, was

introduced for fast, heavy, long distance goods trains and express mixed traffic, and since that date the stock of this useful locomotive has been considerably augmented.

In 1920 the Great Western Railway purchased twenty 2–8–0 engines from the Government for goods services, and the following year placed a contract with Messrs. R. Stephenson & Co., Darlington, for the construction of thirty-five G.W.R. standard 2–6–0 engines.

The amalgamations, which included practically the whole of the Welsh railways, and were effected as a

Vale of Rheidol Locomotive, 1 ft. 11½ in. Gauge

result of the Railways Act, 1921, increased the Great Western Railway's stock of locomotives, and as and when these engines have passed through the shops, they have been brought as far as is practicable into line with Great Western Railway standards.

Among other railways taken over by the Great Western Railway was the Vale of Rheidol line, which runs from Aberystwyth to Devil's Bridge, a length of 11¾ miles. It

P=Passenger **G**=Goods **M**=Mixed Traffic **B**=Branch

See last column

Date	CLASS: Name	CLASS: No.	Type	CYLINDERS: No.	CYLINDERS: Dia. and Stroke	Boiler Pressure lbs. per sq. in.	Diameter of Coupled Wheels	
					in. in.		ft. in.	
1895	Duke	3252	4-4-0	2 ins.	18 × 26	165	5 8	**P**
1896		36	4-6-0	2 ins.	20 × 24		4 7½	**G**
1897	Badminton	4100	4-4-0	2 ins.	18 × 26		6 8½	**P**
1898	Bulldog	3312	4-4-0	2 ins.	18 × 26	165	5 8	**P**
1899	Kruger	2601	4-6-0	2 ins.	19 × 28	180	4 7½	**G**
1900		2600	2-6-0	2 ins.	18 × 26	200	4 7½	**G**
1900	Atbara	4120	4-4-0	2 ins.	18 × 26	180	6 8½	**P**
1901		2602	2-6-0	2 ins.	19 × 28	165	4 7½	**G**
1902	William Dean	2900	4-6-0	2 outs.	18 × 30	200	6 8½	**P**
1903		2611	2-6-0	2 ins.	18 × 26	200	4 7½	**G**
1903		3100	2-6T-2	2 outs.	18 × 30	195	5 8	**M**
1903	City of Bath	3710	4-4-0	2 ins.	18 × 26	195	6 8½	**P**
1903	Ernest Cunard	2998	4-6-0	2 outs.	18 × 30	200	6 8½	**P**
1903	La France (purchased)	102	4-4-2	4 { 2 hp. / 2 lp. } comp'nd	$13\frac{3}{8} \times 25\frac{3}{16}$ / $22\frac{1}{16} \times 25\frac{3}{16}$	227	6 8½	**P**
1903	Albion	2971	4-6-0	2 outs.	18 × 30	200	6 8½	**P**
1904	Albion converted to	2971	4-4-2	2 outs.	18 × 30	200	6 8½	**P**
1904	County of Middlesex	3800	4-4-0	2 outs.	18 × 30	200	6 8½	**P**
1904		4400	2-6T-2	2 outs.	16½ × 24	165	4 1½	**G**
1905	Alliance & President (purchased)	103 & 104	4-4-2	4 { 2 hp. / 2 lp. } comp'nd	$14\frac{3}{16} \times 25\frac{3}{16}$ / $23\frac{5}{8} \times 25\frac{3}{16}$	227	6 8½	**P**
1905		2801	2-8-0	2 outs.	18 × 30	200	4 7½	**G**
1905	County Tank	2221	4-4T-2	2 outs.	18 × 30	195	6 8½	**P**
1905	Ivanhoe	2981	4-4-2	2 outs.	18 × 30	225	6 8½	**P**
1906	Krugers converted to		2-6-0	2 ins.	18 × 26	200	4 7½	**G**
1906	Lady Superior	2901	4-6-0	2 outs.	18 × 30	225	6 8½	**P**
1906	North Star	4000	4-4-2	4	14 × 26	225	6 8½	**P**
1906		4500	2-6T-2	2 outs.	17 × 24	180	4 7½	**G**
1907		2821	2-8-0	2 outs.	$18\frac{3}{8}$ × 30	225	4 7½	**G**
1907	Albion reconverted to	2971	4-6-0	2 outs.	18 × 30	225	6 8½	**P**
1907	Dog Star	4001	4-6-0	4	14¼ × 26	225	6 8½	**P**
1907	25—'s converted to	3901	2-6T-2	2 outs.	17½ × 24	200	5 2	**M**
1907	Prairie Tank	3151	2-6T-2	2 outs.	18½ × 30	200	5 8	**G**
1908	The Great Bear	111	4-6-2	4	15 × 26	225	6 8½	**P**
1908	Auricula (Flowers)	4101	4-4-0	2 ins.	18 × 26	195	6 8½	**P**
1909	Blackbird	3441	4-4-0	2 ins.	18 × 26	195	5 8	**P**
1909	North Star converted	4000	4-6-0	4	14¼ × 26	225	6 8½	**P**
1910	Consolidation Tank	4201	2-8T-0	2 outs.	18½ × 30	200	4 7½	**G**
1911		2831	2-8-0	2 outs.	18½ × 30	225	4 7½	**G**
1911		4301	2-6-0	2 outs.	18½ × 30	200	5 8	**M**
1912	Ivanhoe converted to	2981	4-6-0	2 outs.	18 × 30	225	6 8½	**P**
1913		4530	2-6T-2	2 outs.	17 × 24	200	4 7½	**G**
1913		4600	4-6T-2	2 outs.	17 × 24	200	5 8	**B**
1913	Prince of Wales	4041	4-6-0	4	15 × 26	225	6 8½	**P**
1919		4700	2-8-0	2 outs.	19 × 30	225	5 8	**M**
1923		5205	2-8T-0	2 outs.	19 × 30	200	4 7½	**M**
1923	Caerphilly Castle	4073	4-6-0	4	16 × 26	225	6 8½	**P**

has a gauge of 1 ft. 11½ in. only, and two new locomotives for this railway were built at Swindon in 1923.

Here is a statement covering the period from 1895 to date, which gives the years in which the first engines of various kinds were constructed, and shews the number of cylinders, their diameter and stroke, boiler pressure, and diameters of coupled wheels. This statement briefly summarises Great Western Railway locomotive history over the period.

Mr. C. B. Collett succeeded Mr. Churchward as Chief Mechanical Engineer in 1922, and the outstanding incident in British locomotive practice in the following year was the production of his "Caerphilly Castle."

And now we will have a chat about that wonderful locomotive, and her sister engines.

CHAPTER THE FIFTH

THE MOST POWERFUL LOCOMOTIVE

BRITAIN's most powerful express passenger engine No. 4073, "Caerphilly Castle," made her debut at Paddington Station on August 23, 1923. The engine (4-cylinder 4–6–0 type) was built at the Great Western Railway Locomotive Works, Swindon, and nine sister engines have since "come out." They are named :

4074. Caldicot Castle
4075. Cardiff Castle.
4076. Carmarthen Castle.
4077. Chepstow Castle.
4078. Pembroke Castle.
4079. Pendennis Castle.
4080. Powderham Castle.
4081. Warwick Castle.
4082. Windsor Castle.

"Caerphilly Castle" is a development of the "Star" Class and possesses several new and distinctive departures. She carries larger cylinders (diameter 16 in., stroke 26 in.), and to supply them with steam a new boiler has been designed. While retaining the special features of the G.W.R. standard boiler, the dimensions have been increased, the barrel being 5ft. $1\frac{15}{16}$ in. in diameter at the front end and 5 ft. 9 in. at the throat plate, the length remaining at 14 ft. 10 in. as in the case of the No. 1 standard boiler.

DIAGRAM OF G.W.R. FOUR-CYLINDER (4-6-0) "CASTLE" CLASS LOCOMOTIVE

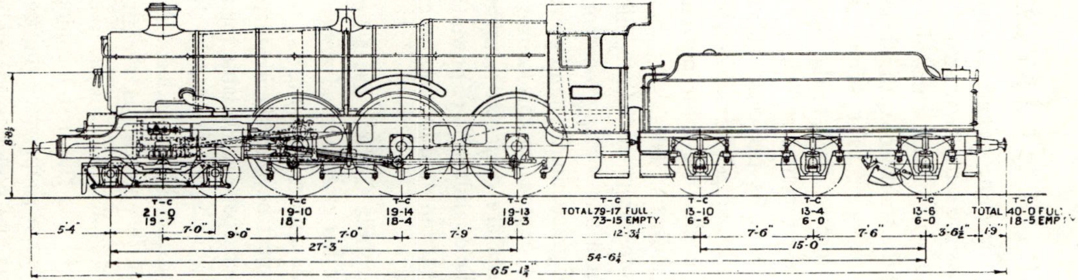

DESCRIPTION

CYLINDERS (FOUR)—Dia., 16″; Stroke, 26″; Steam ports, 25″ by 1¼″; Exhaust 25″ by 3″.

BOILER—Barrel, 14′ 10″; Dia. Outs. 5′ 9″ and 5′ $1\frac{15}{16}$″.

FIREBOX—Outside 10′ 0″ by 6′ 0″; 4′ 0″;
Inside, 9′ $2\frac{7}{16}$″ by 5′ 0¼″; 3′ $2\frac{5}{8}$″;
Height, 6′ 8⅜″ and 5′ 3⅞″.

TUBES

Superheater tubes, No. 84, Dia., 1″; length, 15′ 3⅜″
Fire tubes, No. 201, Dia., 2″; No. 14, Dia., 5⅛″; length, 15′ $2\frac{7}{16}$″.

HEATING SURFACE

Superheater tubes	..	262·62 sq. ft.	Total 2312·0 sq. ft
Fire tubes ..	.. ..	1,885·62 sq. ft.	
Fireboxes ..	.. ..	163·76 sq. ft.	

AREA OF FIREGRATE—30·28 sq. ft.

WHEELS—Bogie, 3′ 2″; Coupled, 6′ 8½″.

WATER CAPACITY OF TENDER—3,500 gallons

WORKING PRESSURE—225 lb. sq. in.

TRACTIVE EFFORT—31,625 lb.

The fire-box is of the same design as that fitted to No. 7 standard, and has the same grate area. The inside cylinders are supplied with steam through passages in the saddle supporting the smoke-box, the steam pipes for the outside cylinders being brought through the side of the smoke-box and connected direct to the steam chests.

The provision of larger cylinders brings the tractive effort up to 31,625 lb. at 85 per cent. boiler pressure, compared with 27,800 lb. of the former 4-cylinder class, thus making the new engine the most powerful express passenger engine in the British Isles.

Here are some photographs of " Caerphilly Castle," and you will see what a fine looking locomotive she is, a veritable blending of grace, dignity, and power. There are larger and heavier engines in this country, but the work for which engines are designed is to haul trains. " Tractive effort " is the qualification of power, and it is in tractive effort that this triumph in locomotive engineering excels.

You will see " Caerphilly Castle " has a longer frame than former engines of her class, and advantage has been taken of this to provide a more roomy cab. None of the fittings in the cab project beyond the regulator handle, so that greatly increased space is available for the engine crew. Additional windows are provided in the cab and the roof has been considerably extended. A feature of the " Castle " Class of locomotives is the provision of tip-up seats for both driver and fireman.

" Caerphilly Castle " was the first locomotive to be turned out of the Swindon shops since the war with the artistic lined-out panels and boiler bands, polished brass

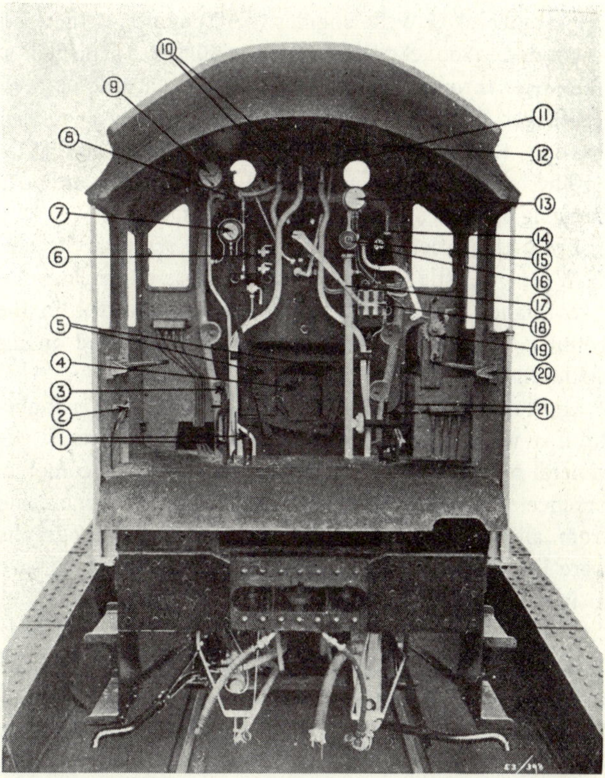

Cab of " Castle " Class Locomotive shewing Controls, etc.

1—Damper Controls
2—Coal Watering Cock
3—Exhaust Injector Control
4—Flap Plate
5—Firehole Doors
6—Water Gauge
7—Steam-Heating Pressure Gauge
8—Steam Heating Valve
9—Boiler Steam Pressure Gauge
10—Exhaust Injector Live Steam Cocks
11—Right-hand Injector (Steam)
12—Condensing Pipes for Lubricator
13—Vacuum Gauge
14—Ejector Steam Valve
15—Ejector Air Valve
16—Blower Valve
17—Regulator Handle
18—Lubricator
19—Reversing Handle
20—Tip-up Seat
21—Sanding Gear Levers

cab and splasher beadings which add so much to the smart appearance of G.W.R. engines. All engines of the 4000, 2900 and 3800 classes will be similarly furnished as they pass through Swindon shops, so that the express passenger engines will soon be as smart as ever they were.

The weight of "Caerphilly Castle" and tender in working order is approximately 120 tons.

From this brief description you will see that the new G.W.R. "Castle" Class of express passenger locomotives stands pre-eminent as the most powerful in the country, and Mr. Collett is to be congratulated on his achievement.

Until the appearance of "Caerphilly Castle," it is doubtful if it was generally appreciated how much interest the general public, young and old, take in British locomotive practice. Demands for photographs of the engine came from all quarters. Publishers of railway photographs were literally inundated with orders, from postcard size to immense enlargements from railway enthusiasts from "China to Peru." Quite a number of railwayists have ordered large hand-coloured photographs, and one keen enthusiast has gone so far as to have a weather vane of the engine made in copper and accurately coloured, which he has had mounted on top of an aerial mast in the West of England.

Reproductions of the engine, with others, have also appeared upon cigarette cards, and doting fathers, uncles, and big brothers, are now consuming a special brand of cigarette in the fond hope of finding enclosed in the packet a "Caerphilly," which is not unnaturally, perhaps, regarded as a sort of prize card of the series by their "young hopefuls."

Thousands of jig-saw puzzles of the engine have been sold and the invitation to "Build the Caerphilly Castle" has met with a wonderful response.

As already stated, "Caerphilly Castle" has been taken to the British Empire Exhibition where she is on view on the Great Western Railway Company's stand in the Palace of Engineering. Since the opening of the Exhibition in April last there has been practically a continuous stream of visitors waiting to go into the cab and inspect this wonderful locomotive.

CHAPTER THE SIXTH

CLASSES, TYPES, NUMBERS, AND NAMES

As you already know, there are three main classes of locomotives—passenger, goods, and shunting—and these may be subdivided into:

PASSENGER: express, semi-express, stopping, suburban or branch trains.

GOODS: fast vacuum fitted, ordinary goods and mineral trains.

SHUNTING: for work in goods yards and docks.

A passenger engine may on occasion be required to work a goods train; a shunting engine, a local passenger train, and so forth. The need for a locomotive which will satisfactorily haul a passenger or goods train has led to the production of the very useful " mixed traffic " type.

The nature of the traffic, the speed at which the train has to run, the weight of the load, and the character of the road (gradients, etc.) are all factors which have to be taken into consideration by the locomotive designer.

You have already made the acquaintance of the numeral system of classifying engines by their wheel arrangement. This system, which hails from America, is now almost universal. It is known as the " Whyte " numeral classification. You will recall that the three numerals in their order, beginning with the front of the engines, signify, first, the leading or carrying wheels, a pair (pony truck) or four (bogie) ; the second numeral indicates the number of driving or coupled wheels ; and the last numeral represents the number of carrying wheels or trailers behind the drivers.

Thus, 4–6–0 represents a ten-wheeled engine with a leading bogie (4 wheels), six coupled driving wheels and no trailing wheels—4 + 6 + 0 = 10.

This system of classification takes no account of the tender, but the letter T is added to distinguish tank engines—thus : 2–8–0T.

Locomotives may be classified, according to their wheel arrangements, into the following four main groups :

1. All wheels coupled.
2. Carrying wheels in front of coupled wheels.
3. Carrying wheels behind coupled wheels.
4. Carrying wheels in front of and behind coupled wheels.

I will give you a brief description of some of the G.W.R. engines in each of these classes, and here are photographs of various types which you can examine meanwhile.

ALL WHEELS COUPLED TOGETHER

The types of engine in this group consist mainly of 0–4–0T (4-wheel coupled tank engines), 0–6–0T (6-wheel coupled tank engines) for shunting, etc., and

0–8–0 (8-wheel coupled) engines for freight and mineral traffic main line work. This wheel arrangement is particularly suitable for moving heavy loads, as the whole of the weight of the engine is available for adhesion.

0-6-0T Shunting Engine

Engines of this type are designed with smaller diameter wheels to give the necessary tractive force, and this makes them unsuitable for fast running.

CARRYING WHEELS IN FRONT OF COUPLED WHEELS

2-4-0. These are 4-wheel coupled engines, with a leading pair of carrying wheels. This type is still used to some extent for passenger traffic.

2-6-0. These engines (6-wheel coupled with a leading pony truck) are usually designed with 4 ft. $7\frac{1}{2}$ in. diameter wheels for freight work. They have superseded the 6-wheel coupled 0–6–0 engine for this work, and are the outcome of the need for larger boiler capacity to meet the demand for increased power required for present-day heavy loads.

2-8-0 or "Consolidation" type. These tender engines (8-wheel coupled with a leading pony truck) are

2-6-0 "Aberdare" Class

provided with 4 ft. $7\frac{1}{2}$ in. diameter wheels, and are designed for heavy mineral traffic. The extra pair of coupled wheels enables a larger boiler to be carried, and the leading pony truck permits a slightly greater speed than

2-8-0 "Consolidation" "2800" Class

with the 0–8–0 engine. An example of this type of engine is the 2800 class of the Great Western Railway.

2-8-0T. The 4200 class of Great Western engine represents the "Consolidation" tank engine, and is built on the lines of the 2800 class. It has, however, a smaller boiler and side tanks and bunker instead of a tender. These are extremely useful engines for "banking" purposes, and for moving heavy mineral trains in congested districts.

2-8-0T "Consolidation" "4200" Class

2-6-0 "Mixed Traffic" Engine. This engine is not required to run as fast as the express passenger engine with 6 ft. 8½ in. wheels, and its wheels are, therefore, of medium size (5 ft. 8 in.), which enables a fairly fast speed to be attained on passenger trains and sufficient power

2-6-0 "Mixed Traffic" "4300" Class

to be developed to work fairly heavy freight trains. These engines are particularly useful when there are severe gradients which put fast running out of the question. On the Great Western Railway they are represented by the 4300 class.

2-8-0 "Mixed Traffic" Engine. These engines (4700 class) are exceptional, as they are the only ones of their class in this country with 5 ft. 8 in. coupled wheels. The larger boiler means an increase of weight,

2-8-0 Mixed Traffic "Consolidation" "4700" Class

which is available for the extra adhesion consequent on the extra pair of coupled wheels.

4-4-0 type. These engines (4-wheel coupled with a leading bogie) were for a long time the standard for express passenger work, and are still used for this purpose

4-4-0 "Bulldog" Class

on lines where heavier engines cannot be utilised. They have done splendid work, and with medium loads can still put up some fine performances. Typical 4-4-0 engines are the "City" Class with inside cylinders and the "County" Class with outside cylinders. Both classes have 6 ft. 8½ in. driving wheels. The "County" Class is the more powerful.

4-6-0 type. This important type of engine (6-wheel coupled with leading bogie) has now largely taken the

4-4-0 "County" Class

place of the 4–4–0 for express passenger trains, on account of the adhesion obtained with the additional pair of coupled wheels and the larger boiler which can be carried. The 4-cylinder (4000) class and the 2-cylinder (2900) class on the Great Western are typical examples of this type

4-6-0 (2-cylinder) "2900" Class

of engine. As you know, an engine of the former class covers the 226 miles non-stop from Paddington to Plymouth, our "The 10.30 Limited," in four hours and seven minutes—a feat which conclusively proves the soundness of the locomotive design and its suitability for the work it has to do. "Caerphilly Castle" and her sister engines are the latest development of the 4–6–0 type on the Great Western Railway, and the most powerful passenger train engines in this country.

4-6-0 (4-cylinder) "4000" Class

CARRYING WHEELS BEHIND THE COUPLED WHEELS

Included in this group are the 0–4–2T and 0–6–2T classes of engines. The former was designed for passenger traffic and is still used for this purpose, but increasing loads make these engines unsuitable for main line traffic. Nowadays they are usually employed on branch lines and similar light work.

The 0–6–2T is a development of the 0–6–0T and performs the same duties, the additional pair of trailing carrying wheels having been provided to accommodate a larger bunker and tank. As already mentioned, they are largely used for shunting purposes, in which case their coupled wheels are less than 5 ft. in diameter. Several examples of this type of engine are in service in South Wales.

CARRYING WHEELS IN FRONT OF AND BEHIND COUPLED WHEELS

4-4-2 "Atlantic." This type of passenger engine is another development of the 4–4–0, the trailing pair of

4-4-2 French Compound "Atlantic" Class

carrying wheels being provided to enable a larger boiler to be carried. For climbing stiff gradients the adhesion obtained from the four coupled wheels is not sufficient,

4-4-2T "Atlantic" Tank

and slipping occurs, with consequent loss of running time. The French compound engines are the only examples of this type on the Great Western Railway.

4-4-2T. The "Atlantic" Class are the best known

of the express tank engines. The typical " Atlantic " tank on the Great Western is the 2221 class, used chiefly for suburban passenger traffic.

2-6-2T. This is a powerful six coupled tank engine represented on the Great Western by the 3100 class, which has 5 ft. 8 in. diameter coupled wheels, and can, therefore, be employed on freight and passenger work. It may be classified as a " mixed traffic " tank engine.

2-6-2T " Prairie " Tank " 3100 " Class

These tank engines are usually termed " double enders," as they are designed to run in either direction. By carrying coal and water on the same frame as the engine, the cost of a separate tender is avoided, and as it is not necessary to turn the engine at the end of each journey, much trouble is avoided.

As we have already seen, the earliest of the Great Western Railway locomotives were named. In those days the names were in series, and were selected on a systematic basis in accordance with present-day practice. Just as we have ten representatives of the " Castle " Class to-day, there was a " Star " Class (1837–1841)—consisting of " North Star," " Morning Star," " Evening Star," " Dog Star," etc. ; a " Fire " or " Firefly " Class (1840)—" Firefly," " Spitfire," " Wild Fire," " Fireball," etc. ; and a " Sun " Class (1840–1841) —" Sun," " Sunbeam," " Meridian," " Comet," etc. All these and other broad gauge locomotives were named but not numbered, but some years later numbers were allotted, and this became standard practice for all engines.

With the exception of certain of the famous 7 ft. singles, however, narrow gauge engines were not named until 1892, the year of the gauge conversion, when names were again introduced on Mr. Dean's celebrated 7 ft. 8 in. singles, and from this time onwards passenger train engines were given names in addition to numbers. It is interesting to note that, as names were again introduced, a number of engines were christened after some of the old broad gauge engines.

Goods engines are numbered, but not now named.

The locomotive with a name has something of a personality which a mere number cannot supply, and there is much to be said for naming engines quite apart from the fact that it appeals to the travelling public. In the workshops, when a particular part for a " Star " or " County " is asked for, it is immediately identified, and in referring to, say, the boiler, one is helped to recall immediately that a " Court " carries a standard No. 1, a " City " a standard No. 4 boiler, and so on.

Frequently, engines to which names are not appropriated are christened by common consent as soon as they go into service, and an example of this is the " Aberdares " (2–6–0 goods). This is a further indication of the usefulness of naming engines.

There are other class names in use which are American in origin, such as "Pacific"—4–6–2, "Atlantic"—4–4–2, "Consolidation"—2–8–0, "Prairie"—2–6–2, "Mogul"—2–6–0, etc.

As you doubtless know, many youthful and other railway enthusiasts take a keen interest in the names, numbers, types, and classes of locomotives, and for their assistance a little booklet, "Great Western Railway Engines," * has been compiled, giving the names, etc., of the Company's locomotives.

Here is a table giving examples of the types, classes, name series, or numbers of G.W.R. locomotives. You may look in vain for "The Great Bear," the G.W.R. giant engine, and the first "Pacific" locomotive (4–6–2) to be built in this country. This engine achieved almost world-wide notoriety by reason of the fact that she was the largest and heaviest locomotive running on the Great Western Railway. Built in 1908, she had a tractive effort of 27,800 lb. and weighed 142 tons 15 cwt. Since "The Great Bear" came into being, however, the "Castle" Class of 4–6–0 engines has been evolved and has proved most successful. The latter type of engine weighs only 119 tons 17 cwt., but has a tractive effort of 31,625 lb. "The Great Bear" is, therefore, outclassed both in power and weight. She recently went into the shops at Swindon for general repairs, which include new

* *"Great Western Railway Engines: Names, Numbers, Types, and Classes"* (1s.) *Published by "Great Western Railway Magazine," Paddington Station, London, W. 2.*

EXAMPLES OF LOCOMOTIVE CLASSIFICATION BY WHEEL ARRANGEMENT

Type	*Size of Wheels*	*Classes—Passenger Numbers—Goods, Mixed Traffic and Branch*
	ft. in.	
4-6-0	6 8½	4-Cylinder
		STARS
		KNIGHTS
		KINGS
		QUEENS
		PRINCES
		PRINCESSES
		ABBEYS
		CASTLES
4-6-0	6 8½	2-Cylinder
		LADY
		SAINT
		COURT
		VARIOUS
4-4-0	6 8½	COUNTY
		ATBARA CITIES
		CITIES
		BADMINTON
		ATBARA
		FLOWERS
	5 8	BULLDOGS, VARIOUS
		DIRECTORS
		PLACE
		PLACE
		BIRDS
		DUKES OR DEVONS
4-4-2	6 8½	4-Cylinder (French Engines)
4-4T-2	6 8½	ATLANTIC TANKS (COUNTY)
	5 8	ATLANTIC TANKS (BRANCH)
2-4-0	6 2	BARNUMS
2-6-0	4 7½	2600–2680
	5 8	4300–4399
		5300–5399
		6300–6361
		6370–6399
		7300–7319
2-6T-2	5 8	3100 & 3111–3190
	5 2	3901–3920
	4 7½	4500–4574
	4 1½	4400–4410
2-8-0	5 8	4700–4708
	4 7½	2800–2883
2-8T-0	4 7½	4200–4299
		5200–5244

cylinders and a new boiler, and arrangements are being made to reconstruct her so that she will be similar to the "Castle" type. As the only Great Western "Pacific," therefore, her last journey has been run. She is to be rechristened "Viscount Churchill."

The "Castle" class having proved very successful and economical, it has been decided to build ten more of them as soon as possible, and to convert the older 4-cylinder engines, which bear the names of "Stars," "Knights," "Kings," "Queens," "Princes" "Princesses" and "Abbeys" to the same type, as and when they require new cylinders and boilers.

CHAPTER THE SEVENTH

SPEED

FROM the earliest days the Great Western Railway earned a name for speed, and in tracing the history of Great Western Railway locomotives, we have referred once or twice to some speedy runs. It is a favourite Great Western tradition that, as far back as 1842 in connection with some speed experiments, " an expert driver ran his train over the 18 miles between London and Slough in 15 minutes," and that in 1848 " the 53 miles between London and Didcot were traversed in 47 minutes." It is stated that on this latter occasion the great Brunel was on the foot-plate of the engine. In the " World Almanac " (an American publication) this record still holds priority of place among a list of " notable fast runs of passenger trains for long distances." The actual entry reads—Date : May, 1848. Railroad : Great Western—England. Terminals : London—Didcot (distance—miles) 53·25. Inclusive time : H. 0. M. 47. (Miles per hour) 68.

For a number of years the Great Western Railway enjoyed the reputation of having the fastest train in the world in its famous " Flying Dutchman." The down train ran from London to Exeter with five intermediate stops, and did the London-Swindon portion at the rate of 53 miles an hour. A railway enthusiast 82 years of age, now domiciled in America, says he well remembers how school-boys of that time (1865) used to gather on the bridges and alongside the line to see this wonderful train pass on its way.

"City of Bath" established a world record on July 14, 1903, when hauling a special train conveying the King and Queen (then Prince and Princess of Wales) to Plymouth.

"City of Bath"

The train of 130 tons was timed to cover the $245\frac{5}{8}$ miles to Plymouth, North Road station, in $4\frac{1}{2}$ hours without a stop, but actually accomplished the trip in 3 hours $53\frac{1}{2}$ minutes, or at an average speed of 63 miles an hour! The route taken on this occasion was via Bristol, $19\frac{1}{4}$ miles longer than that via Westbury. The shortened route to the West was opened in 1906.

It was a sister engine, No. 3440 "City of Truro," now No. 3717, which, on a wonderful run with ocean mails from Plymouth to Bristol in May 1904, reached a speed of over 100 miles an hour as timed by the late Mr. Rous

Marten, a recognised authority on train speeds. This wonderful record was kept a secret for eighteen years.*

If you have not done so, you should certainly study the log of this train, which reveals some really remarkable speeds, apart from the wonderful record set up. As a result of this record run, American, New Zealand and Australian mails, brought to Plymouth by s.s. *Kronprinz Wilhelm*, were delivered in London 5 days 21 hours 58 minutes from the time of their departure from New York!

" Duke of Connaught "

As I have already stated, the engine from Plymouth to Bristol was " City of Truro," and from Bristol to London the train was hauled by No. 3065, " Duke of Connaught," one of Mr. Dean's 7 ft. 8 in. single wheelers. Although " City of Truro " did such wonderful running, it is interesting to note that the following average speeds were made by " Duke of Connaught " after leaving Bristol East Depot:

Bristol, East Depot to Bath	60·78 m.p.h.
Bath to Swindon	68·35 ,,
Swindon to Didcot	74·28 ,,
Didcot to Reading	78·88 ,,
Reading to Paddington	79·17 ,,

* *Mr. Rous Marten's own account of this run is quoted at length in " The* 10.30 *Limited."*

The run of 118 miles 33 chains from Bristol (Pylle Hill) to Paddington was accomplished in 99 minutes 46 seconds to the final stop at Paddington platform. Mr. Rous Marten said at the time that "Duke of Connaught" behaved admirably throughout the whole distance, and reached Paddington "perfectly cool in every bearing, tight in every tube and joint, entirely fit for an immediate run back to Bristol had this been desired." This engine did actually return to Bristol with an express train two hours after its arrival with the mail train at Paddington.

In April 1905 two outstanding non-stop runs were made. "County of Devon" put up a record for a trip from Plymouth to Birmingham via Bristol and Oxford, 267 miles. A special Cunard boat train, with a load of 400 tons behind the tender, made a remarkable run from Fishguard Harbour to London, and covered the 100 miles from Badminton to Paddington in 87 minutes.

On July 21, 1906, the regular Cornish Riviera express service was commenced with the longest non-stop run in the world from Paddington to Plymouth,* a record which has been held for the past eighteen years. Although its fine time of 4 hours 7 minutes for the journey is sometimes beaten by ocean mail trains from Plymouth to Paddington, yet year in and year out this "wonder train to the west," familiarly known as "The 10.30 Limited," traverses the 226 miles with clockwork regularity; in fact, it is said that in the towns and villages through which it passes folks take their time from the "Limited." You, however, already

* *The year* 1904 *saw the introduction of a non-stop service between Paddington and Plymouth, which for two years ran in the summer season only.*

know something of this wonderful train, its luxurious appointments and unique record of punctuality and having

Cornish Riviera Express

so recently made the trip to the west by "The 10.30 Limited," you can understand why it is the most popular train in the time-table.

There have been a number of other fine runs from time to time, but not to weary you unduly we will now skip to 1923, and see some of the recent achievements. The outstanding feature of that year was a Paddington to Plymouth North Road non-stop run of "The 10.30 Limited" (divided) in four hours exactly. Paddington to Birmingham (110¼ miles), with a three minutes stop at Leamington, was accomplished in two hours, and no longer time was occupied in doing Paddington to Bristol and *vice versa*.

The service between Paddington and Birmingham is worthy of special notice, constituting as it does the shortest route between England's great centres of industry. Fourteen trains, completing the journey in exactly two hours, are run to and from Birmingham each week-day, and three on Sundays, all equipped with Restaurant Cars.

On July 9, 1923, the Great Western Railway set up yet

another record inaugurating the fastest train in the British Empire and possibly the fastest " start to stop " run in the world. The train is booked to run from Swindon to Paddington ($77\frac{1}{4}$ miles) in 75 minutes, with an average speed of 61·8 miles an hour.

Fastest Train in Kingdom—80 Miles an Hour near Acton

On the first day this train, hauled by engine No. 2915, " Saint Bartholomew," did the trip from Swindon to London in 72 minutes. On a later occasion it attained a speed of 74 miles an hour within the first 5 miles from Swindon, and accelerated to 79 miles an hour farther on the journey.

We are going to see locomotives in course of construction at Swindon Works, and we really must make a point of timing our tour so as to return to London by this fastest train, the 3.45 P.M. from Swindon.

You will be interested to know that the Great Western Railway 1924 summer time-table provides for no less than twenty-nine daily non-stop runs of over one hundred miles !

Talking of records and long runs, you may wonder how many miles one of these modern locomotives can run without going into the shops for overhaul. Engine No. 4041, "Prince of Wales," holds the Great Western record in this respect. The average for this class of engine is 120,000 miles, but "Prince of Wales" has done 163,000 miles on express trains between her (or is it "his"?) visits to the shops.

In view of the really wonderful speeds which have been achieved, you will not unnaturally ask if such fast running is likely to become general, or if there is likely to be any further considerable increase in train speeds.

Well, you must bear in mind that for very fast running favourable conditions are necessary. There must be, of course, a clear road, and with the increased traffic congestion this is a difficult thing to ensure. High speed is not possible when the permanent way is under repair, or on a section of line where there are any sharp curves or steep gradients. Climatic conditions, particularly in a country like ours, are often a serious deterrent to fast running. Fogs and snow are not conducive to speed, and high wind may seriously affect the running of a train.

You must remember too that we live in a densely populated country with a town for about every ten miles of railway. All these towns have to be served by the railways, and as it takes a mile or so for an engine to attain any really high speed you will realise that very fast running is hardly possible for other than long distance non-stop trains.

Comparison between the time-tables of twenty-five to thirty years ago and those of to-day will shew that the average speed of the fastest trains between London and such places as Bristol and Birmingham has risen from 40 or 45 miles an hour to practically 60 miles an hour. Closer investigation, however, will shew that it is rather in maintaining an almost unvarying speed than in any considerable increase in maximum speed that the two hour runs between such places have been possible.

The satisfactory speeds on the Great Western Railway to-day may, I think, be attributed to the continuous improvement in locomotives, the excellent permanent way, the perfecting of signalling and brake gear, and the elimination of stops for water, due to the extended provision of water troughs.

It must be borne in mind, however, that apart from the improvements in speed, the loads of trains have continuously increased, and the load behind the engine is, of course, a very important factor for consideration when making speed comparisons.

The modern locomotive must be capable not only of hauling vastly increased loads at, say, 60 miles an hour on the level, but must also be able to accelerate rapidly so as to regain high speed after a signal or other stop. It must also climb banks of 1 in 200 without considerable reduction in running speed.

"Time is money" is a truism in these days if ever it was, and in the provision of speedy train services the Great Western Railway must have saved its patrons in the aggregate a veritable king's ransom.

CHAPTER THE EIGHTH

ENGINE PARTS

FOR our purposes the locomotive may be roughly divided into three parts: the undercarriage or chassis, i.e. the framing and wheels; the engine, i.e. steam-chests, cylinders, and motion; and the boiler, including fire-box, smoke-box, etc.

The undercarriage requires little description, and in the course of our run on "The 10.30 Limited" it was explained that tractive force is the force exerted at the driving wheels, and that adhesive force depends upon the weight on the driving wheels. You will appreciate that coupling wheels together increases adhesion, and for this reason goods engines have many wheels coupled, so as to distribute the weight of the engine over the driving wheels. The smaller wheels increase tractive force, and this is why driving wheels of goods engines are generally 4 ft. 7½ in. in diameter, and mixed traffic engines (passenger and goods) 5 ft. 8 in. in diameter, whereas fast passenger trains have driving wheels of 6 ft. 8½ in. in diameter.

Now just a word or two about a few of the more important parts of the engine. We shall have something to say about their various functions when considering locomotive operation, or "how it works."

ENGINE PARTS

CYLINDERS

When cylinders are placed outside the frames of the locomotive a separate steam-chest is required for each cylinder. So we find in G.W.R. standard outside 2-cylinder engines two iron castings bolted together, each embodying one cylinder, one steam-chest, and (as the smoke-box saddle or support is a component) half the saddle.

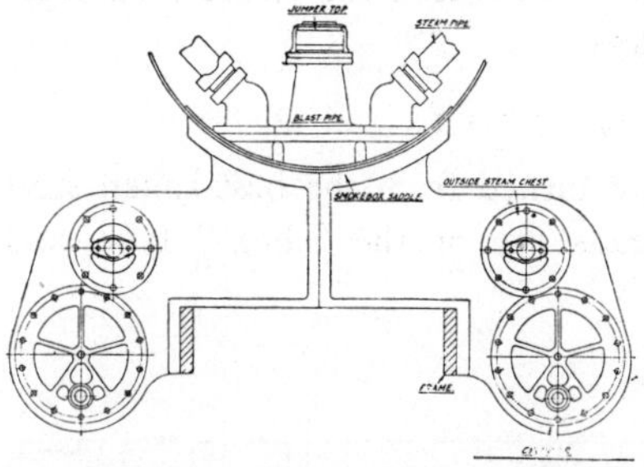

These castings are placed astride the frames to which they are bolted, the cylinders and steam chests being outside.

In the case of the inside cylinders whether of 4-cylinder or of 2-cylinder engines, being nearer together, one common chest is adopted, in which two valves operate. One casting embraces the steam-chest, together with the two cylinders and the smoke-box saddle, or, in the case of the 4-cylinder locomotive, the front part of the saddle, the whole casting being

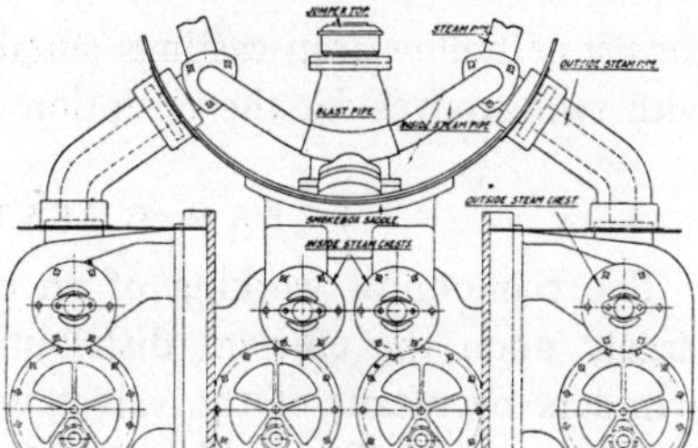

bolted between the frames. The outside cylinders and steam-chests of the 4-cylinder engines are contained in two other castings, which are bolted on the outside of the frames. The rear half of the saddle on the 4-cylinder engine forms a separate casting bolted between the frames, in which is embraced the exhaust passages of the outside cylinders.

PISTONS

The piston rods are turned from the best rolled steel bar. The piston heads are of the "box" type, and

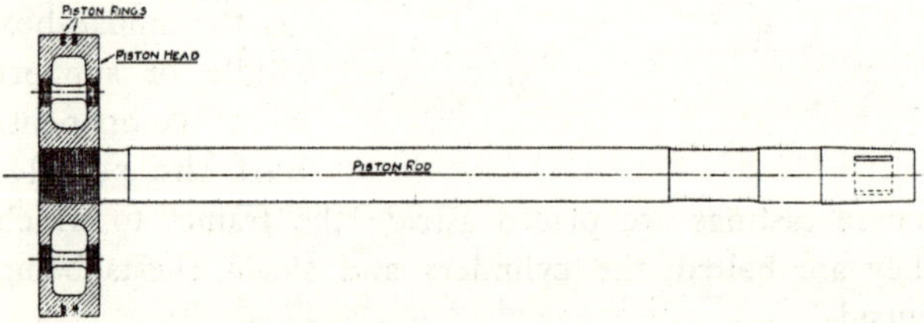

consist of hollow iron castings suitably machined to size, with two grooves for the reception of the piston rings.

STEAM-CHESTS

The economical working of an engine depends very largely upon the efficient distribution of steam to the cylinders by means of the valves which open and close ports or passages for the flow of steam.

The steam-chests are situated above the cylinders and each contains two (or four, if a common steam-chest) cylindrical bushes, which form the housings of the piston valves. Two ports are formed in each bush; the smaller one in each case is connected either to the front or back ends of the cylinder by suitable passages. Between the bushes is the space into which the steam is led from the superheater by copper pipes and passages in the castings. The outer and larger port of each bush opens into a passage leading to the base of the blast pipe, through which the exhaust steam passes from the cylinders.

CONNECTING RODS

The connecting rods, which transmit the motion of the crosshead to the crank pin, are machined from the best forged steel. The dimensions are determined only after most carefully calculating the alternate compression and tensile stresses, and the bending strains to which the rod will be subjected in working. In providing for these it is desirable that the weight of a connecting rod should be kept to a minimum.

COUPLING RODS

Coupling rods are the means of harnessing the adhesive weight of the engine, in order that the tractive effort may be distributed over two or more axles. The coupling rods, like connecting rods, are machined from forged steel of the highest quality.

CROSSHEADS

The crosshead is generally machined from a steel forging, as also the slippers. The bearing surfaces of the latter are lined with white metal. The inside crossheads of the 4-cylinder engines, however, are steel castings, the slippers being an integral part thereof.

DRIVING AXLE-BOXES

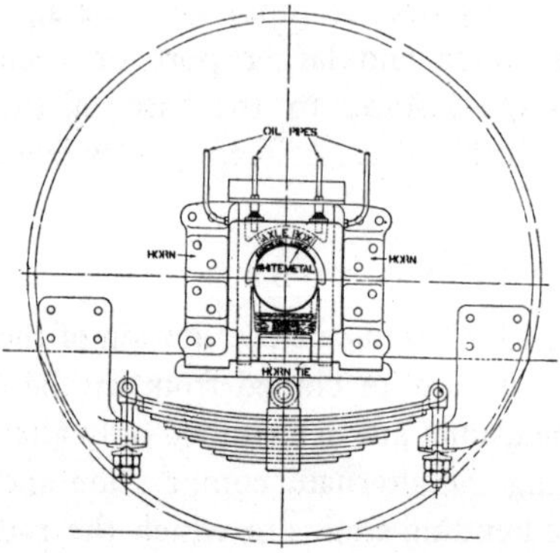

These are steel castings machined to receive gun metal liners upon which are cast white metal bearing surfaces. Four oil pipes are used for lubricating the horns and top of the journal, and a spring lubricating pad supplies oil to the underside of the journal.

INJECTORS

The injector is a means of feeding hot water into the boiler against the steam pressure therein. Two injectors are situated below the footplate, one on either side of the engine. They are operated from the foot-plate above by handles attached to rods.

For locomotive purposes there are two types: live steam restarting injectors, and exhaust restarting injectors. The former is worked by live steam only from the boiler and is fitted on the right-hand side of all G.W.R. engines.

The exhaust injector utilises exhaust steam from the cylinders in conjunction with a small supply from the boiler. If desired this injector can also be worked by live steam alone. It is fitted on the left-hand side of all express passenger engines, and large type goods engines. When no exhaust injector is fitted, two similar live steam restarting injectors are used. The action of both injectors is the same; the steam is passed through a small tapering nozzle, so forming a steam jet of high velocity. This jet is led through a conical water space, where the

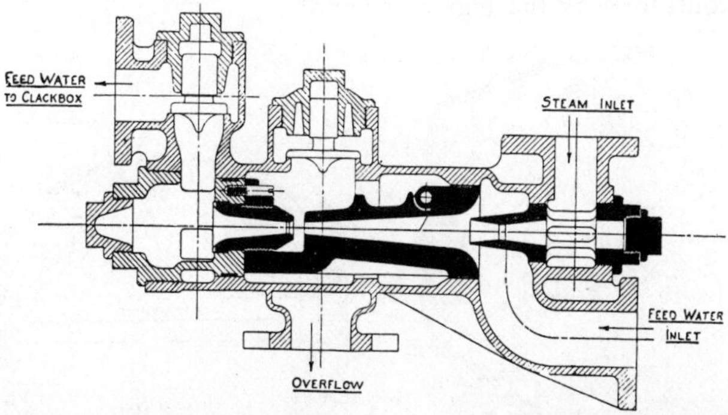

steam is condensed, causing a vacuum in the body of the injector which imparts high velocity to the subsequent column of water. This column of water then passes through a delivery cone of increasing diameter, with which the velocity, or rather what our technical friends more correctly term the "kinetic energy" of the water, changes to pressure, ultimately sufficient to overcome the boiler pressure and to open what is called the "clack" valve in the feed pipe to the boiler.

LUBRICATORS

Now kindly take these two diagrams which show firebox and smoke-box front views of the Swindon improved triple sight feed lubricator, and I will endeavour to explain the action of this ingenious device. Lubrication is effected by feeding cylinder oil into the steam in the regulator-box and in the steam pipes between the superheater and steam-chest by which it is carried in the form of spray to the surfaces to be lubricated. It is controlled by the regulator handle.

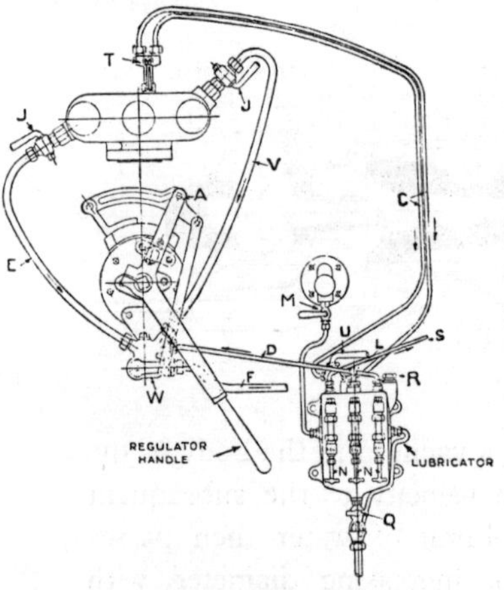

No. 1

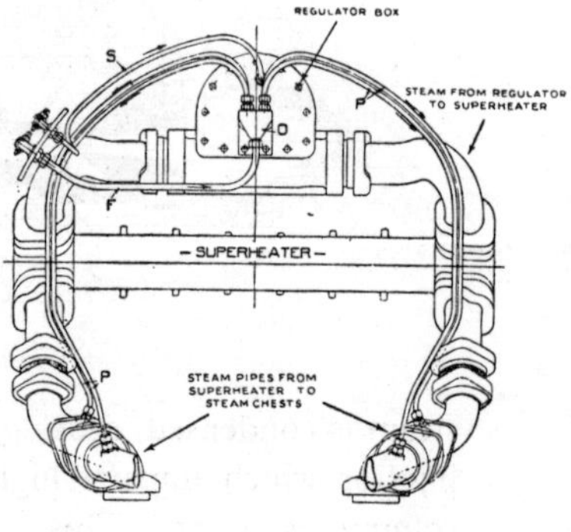

No. 2

The lubricator gives three feeds: one to the regulator-box in the smoke-box, and two, one of which is spare, through valve W in diagram (1) to a distributor O, diagram (2), in the smoke-box. From this distributor, four copper pipes lead the lubricant into the main steam pipes, through which it passes to the cylinders.

Steam from the boiler condenses in pipes C and, entering the enclosed body of the lubricator as water, displaces oil therein through the sight feeds into pipes S and D, diagram (1).

Pipe S leads direct to the regulator-box, diagram (2), but pipe D is connected to valve W, in which the oil is picked up by steam through E and V and carried through pipe F to the distributor O in diagram (2) wherein it is divided into pipes P and so passes into the steam pipes.

In order that a little oil may be fed to the cylinders when coasting or drifting with the regulator shut, and none when the engine is standing, valve W is controlled in a suitable manner direct from the regulator.

The amount of oil passing when the regulator is open depends upon the adjustment of the feed valves N· N, diagram (1).

To warm the oil in cold weather, steam may be passed through the body of the lubricator by opening valve M.

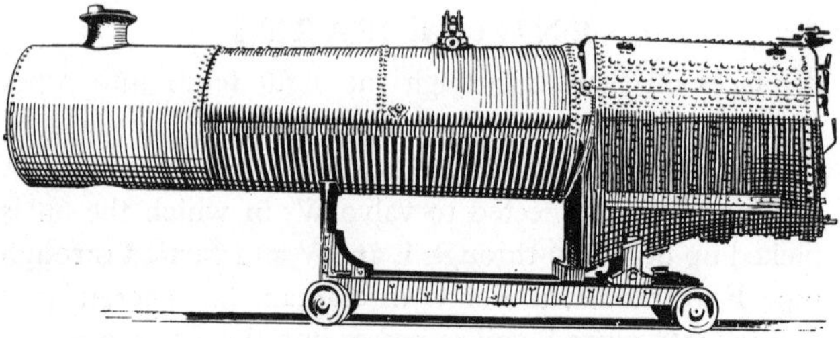

CHAPTER THE NINTH

BOILER PARTS

To the non-technical mind the boiler is, perhaps, the most impressive of the numerous component parts of the locomotive, probably because of its relative size and influence on the general lines of the engine. When speaking of the boiler, we generally include the fire-box, smoke-box, and other adjuncts to the boiler itself.

The principal aims of a boiler designer are to ensure :

1. That the boiler capacity (the amount of steam it is capable of generating in a given time) shall be sufficient to maintain an adequate, but not excessive, supply of steam to meet the requirements of the cylinders under all conditions of working.
2. That every facility for the most economic consumption of the fuel is provided, and that of the total heat of combustion, the maximum shall be transferred to the water and steam.
3. That the boiler will withstand a pressure far in excess of its working pressure.
4. That the dimensions of the boiler will permit the locomotive on which it is mounted conforming to

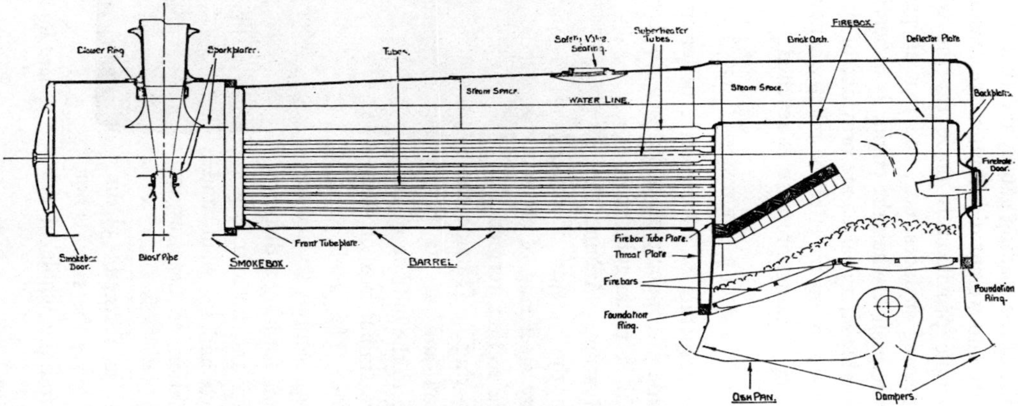

Diagram of Locomotive Boiler

NOTE.—*Superheater, Regulator Box and Gear, Safety Valve, Stays, etc., not shewn.*

the limits of the loading gauge, and that the centre of gravity and weight distribution are reasonable.

5. That ample provision is made for the cleaning of all heating surfaces, etc., and that all parts are readily accessible when the engine is in service.
6. That reliable safety valves are provided of sufficient dimensions to ensure effective relief whenever the maximum working pressure is reached.

FIRE-BOX

The general structure of a locomotive boiler embraces a fire-box made of copper plate about ½ in. in thickness; something like a rectangular box open at the bottom. Around the base and on the outside of this box is a heavy steel ring of about 3½ in. square section, termed the "foundation ring." Outside the entire fire-box and at its base, fitting closely to the outside of the ring, is a very similar box or shell of steel plate. The shell, ring, and fire-box are securely riveted together, the ring forming a distance piece between the bottom edges of the fire-box and its shell, and also a foundation or base, as its name suggests.

Fire-box. No. 7 Standard Boiler

The space so formed (3½ in. immediately above the ring) is not uniform around the whole of the box, but increases slightly with the height, the distance between the top or crown of the fire-box and that of the shell being much greater, for reasons which will be apparent later.

BARREL

The barrel, as may be imagined, is the large horizontal, cylindrical portion, the back end of which is secured to the top portion of the front plate of the fire-box shell. This plate, known as the throat plate, is cut away and arranged to receive it in such a manner as to permit a large area of the fire-box front plate to project above the inside of the barrel.

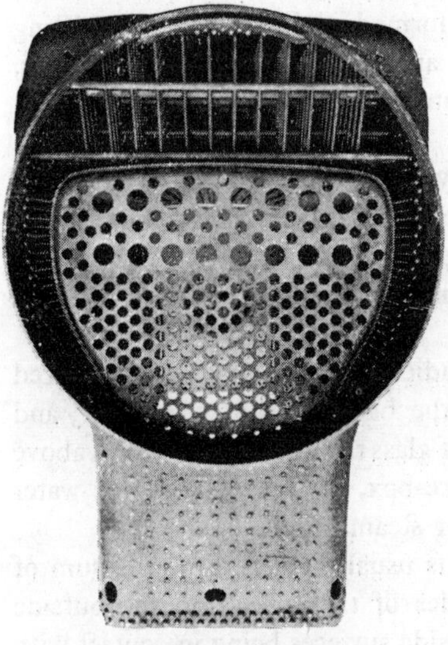

Interior of Fire-box shewing Tube Plate and Stays

The front end of the barrel is sealed by a circular plate riveted in position. This plate and the fire-box front plate are drilled to receive the ends of a large number of steel tubes about 2 in. in diameter, which are inserted between them, both ends of each tube being expanded in the plates to make steam-tight joints. The two plates, for obvious reasons, are termed the tube plates of the boiler.

The barrel and front tube plate are securely stayed or tied to the fire-box and shell by long steel stays, or rods with threaded ends that screw into the plates. The sides and top of the fire-box and shell are similarly stayed to each other by a number of short steel and copper stays.

In approximately the centre of the back plates of the fire-box and shell is formed the fire-hole, consisting generally of a circular aperture 1 ft. 3 in. in diameter, the edges of the plates being pressed and riveted together.

From the foregoing you will realise that the water and steam space in the boiler comprises that between the outside of the tubes and the inside of the barrel, together with the space between the outside of the fire-box and the inside of the shell.

The water level is indicated by a gauge glass secured in a frame bolted on the back plate of the boiler, and positioned so that at half glass the water level is 5 in. above the top of the inside fire-box, the space above the water level being available for steam.

The heating surface is usually taken to be the sum of the areas of the outsides of the tubes and the outside of the fire-box (the outside surfaces being in contact with the water) since the fire is in the latter, and the hot gases pass along the tubes in their progress through the barrel to the smoke-box.

A well-designed boiler permits the natural circulation of the whole of the water it contains when heat is applied.

This is essential to produce good steaming qualities, since all the water must be constantly brought into contact with the heating surfaces and steam generated, in a greater or lesser degree, throughout the whole volume of water, forming bubbles that tend to rise to the surface.

SUPERHEATER

Above the ordinary boiler flue tubes is a row or two rows of larger tubes, and in these are laid the superheater "units." A unit consists of six tubes forming three distinct loops, both ends of which are in a hollow horse-shoe shaped member that is bolted to the "header."

The "header" consists of a large iron casting, resting on brackets and placed transversely across the smokebox, in front of the large superheater tubes. Contained in this casting are two chambers, one for saturated steam and one for superheated steam, connected by copper pipes from the end of the header to the regulator box and the steam-chest respectively—in other words, one to the boiler and the other to the engine. The whole is very accessible and permits easy withdrawal of the units and cleaning of the flue tubes.

You will remember we had something to say about the superheater on our "10.30" trip, and you will recall that saturated steam from the boiler enters the superheater through the regulator valve. Passing from the header it flows into the units, where, in contact with hot unit tubes, it is superheated, and, returning, passes into the chamber of the header connected to the steam-chest,

THE 'SWINDON' SUPER-HEATER

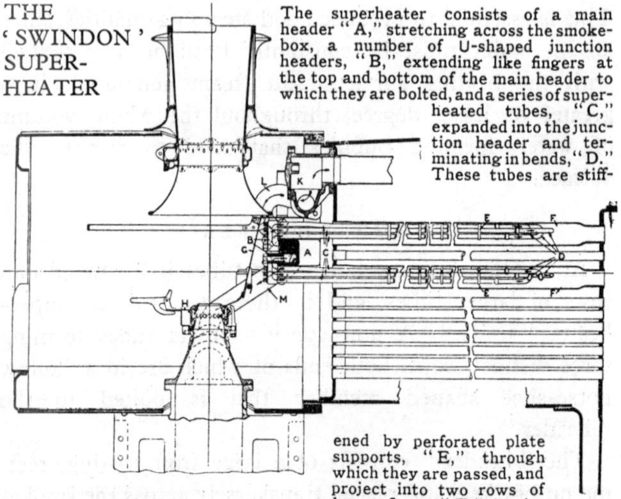

The superheater consists of a main header "A," stretching across the smoke-box, a number of U-shaped junction headers, "B," extending like fingers at the top and bottom of the main header to which they are bolted, and a series of super-heated tubes, "C," expanded into the junction header and terminating in bends, "D." These tubes are stiffened by perforated plate supports, "E," through which they are passed, and project into two rows of large flues, "F," in the boiler. The supports have the additional advantage of disturbing and "churning up" the heated gases as they pass through the flues. The smoke-box portion is enclosed by a casing, "G," the front being hinged to give access to the super-heater, and the bottom is open for the passage of the flue gases under the deflector plate, "H," to the chimney. Steam passes from the boiler through the regulator, "K," and steam pipes, "L," to the top chamber of the main header, "A," thence to one finger of the junction headers, "B," through the small superheater tubes, "C," and bends, "D," to the other finger, thence to the bottom chamber of the header and through the steam pipes, "M," to the cylinders. The course of the steam is indicated by arrows.

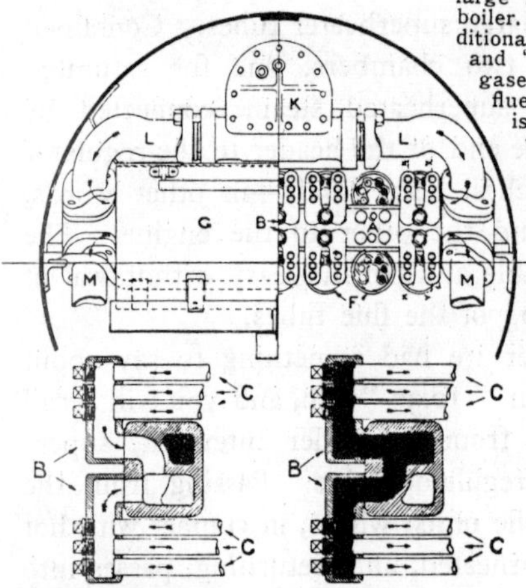

through which, in turn, it passes to the cylinders via the steam ports.

It has already been explained to you how, by increasing the temperature of steam, the superheater reduces the consumption of coal.

Here is a diagram of the most modern type of superheater.

GRATE

The grate is situated at the bottom of the fire-box and consists of one, two, or three sets of cast iron or wrought iron bars resting longitudinally in the box upon transverse rods supported by brackets secured to the underside of the foundation ring. Between the bars is an air space, lugs formed on the ends and middle of the bars acting as distance pieces. Clearance is arranged for the longitudinal expansion of the bars when hot.

Grates are not always horizontal; the foundation ring on the large boilers generally inclines upwards towards the back, although in some cases the inclination is confined to the front end of the box, the back end being horizontal.

ASH-PAN

Under the grate and secured to the foundation ring is an ash-pan of light steel plate, having two, three, or four (according to the size of the grate) hinged doors or dampers operated from the foot-plate above by a series of levers and rods, and arranged to open backwards or forwards according to their position.

The ash-pan thus forms a receptacle in which ashes

from the grate above are trapped (this being particularly necessary when the locomotive is standing) and is also the means of controlling the amount of air admitted to the underside of the grate.

BRICK ARCH

Combustion of a body can only occur providing the surrounding temperature is sufficiently high. It is, therefore, desirable to maintain a high and consistent furnace temperature in the locomotive fire-box. This is aided by the provision of an arch of fire-bricks.

This arch is built above the grate, supported at the fire-box sides and situated immediately adjacent to the tube plate. It is inclined upwards towards the back, the front or tube plate end being just below the bottom row of tubes. The inclination and length of the arch are governed by the area above the top line of the arch and the inside of the fire-box. This must be in correct proportion to the grate area and the total cross sectional area of the tubes, or what is termed the flue area, as the gases pass over the arch in their passage through the boiler.

By so deflecting the gases around the box, the arch assists uniform combustion and renders it more complete. It also, in conjunction with the spark plates in the smoke-box, distributes the gases equally through the tubes.

In order to complete combustion of the gases in the fire-box, it is imperative that a certain amount of air is allowed to have access to the fire-box above the grate. The fire-hole doors are, therefore, cast hollow and open at the bottom with apertures through the inner walls at the top. When the doors are closed, air is drawn up between the walls of each door and through the aperture into the box.

To mix the incoming air thoroughly with the gases, an arched smoke plate or deflector about 20 in. long is fitted in the fire-hole protruding inside the box, so that

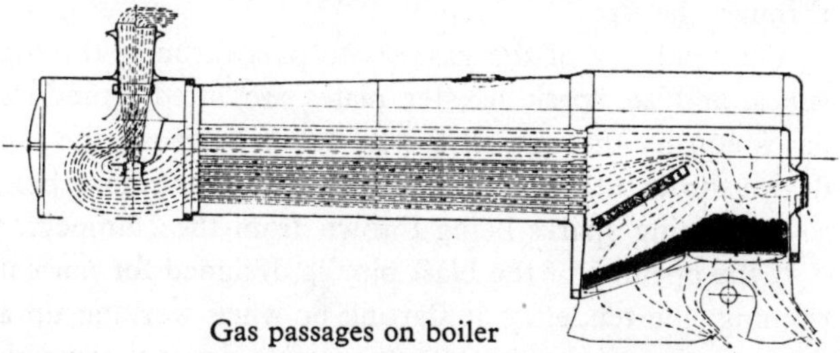

Gas passages on boiler

the air, after passing through the door, is sprayed fanwise into the gases passing around the arch.

SMOKE-BOX

The smoke-box, cylindrical in shape, is situated at the front end of the boiler upon a saddle embodied in the cylinder castings, and formed by a steel wrapper plate riveted to and around the front tube plate and a pressed circular plate carrying an air-tight door of sufficient size to permit cleaning and removal of tubes, etc.

The smoke-box forms an air-tight compartment, with the exception of the chimney orifice, and provides, with its contents, the means of inducing air to enter the firebox in conjunction with the discharge to the atmosphere of the exhaust steam from the cylinders and the waste gases from the furnace.

In the centre of the smoke-box and directly in line with the chimney is situated the blast pipe, through which a large jet of exhaust steam from the cylinders passes with every " beat " of the engine. This jet has sufficient velocity to create a considerable vacuum in the smoke-box, which induces the necessary draught through the fire.

The tendency of the gases is to pass through the top tubes, and so spark arrester plates are fitted to induce gases equally through all the tubes, and deposit the ash drawn through the tubes in the bottom of the smoke-box, so preventing sparks being thrown from the chimney.

If the opening of the blast pipe is designed for normal running, the tendency at starting or when working up a sharp gradient is to create an excessive draught through the fire and back pressure on the pistons, due to the increased volume of the blast. To rectify this an automatic " Jumper " blast pipe top is fitted. This is detachable and has an opening to suit normal conditions. About $2\frac{3}{4}$ in. below the opening a series of sixteen holes is drilled through the pipe, and around the outside, at the top, is formed an inclined seating.

Now take a look at this little diagram. When working heavily, the exhaust steam pressure lifts the ring B, thereby providing an extra outlet for the exhaust through the holes A and the space between the lifted ring B and its seat C, thus relieving the blast. The lift of the ring B is limited by stops. As the pressure becomes normal the ring drops, when the blast pipe orifice is alone in action again. The jumper top can be seen in position in the superheater diagram.

In the smoke-box is also located the regulator box, fixed to the top of the tube plate (containing the main valve and its "jockey" or pilot valve operated from the foot-plate which control the supply of steam from the boiler to the steam-chests); the superheater mounted upon brackets (to which are bolted the heads of the units); the steam pipes connecting the regulator box with the header and the header with the steam-chests of the cylinders.

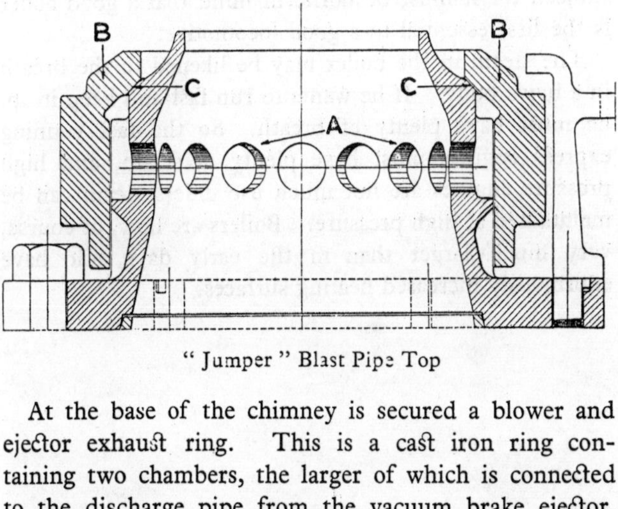

"Jumper" Blast Pipe Top

At the base of the chimney is secured a blower and ejector exhaust ring. This is a cast iron ring containing two chambers, the larger of which is connected to the discharge pipe from the vacuum brake ejector, and the smaller to the steam blower valve. These chambers are situated one above the other, and in each case through the inner wall of the ring is drilled a series of inclined holes, so that the exhaust steam and air from the ejector and live steam from the blower valve are liberated from the respective chambers upwards around the inside opening of the ring. Thus the draught is induced or augmented, the blower only being used when raising steam at the shed, or under exceptional conditions when running.

I am afraid this description of the locomotive boiler, its component parts, and their functions is hardly as brief as I intended it should be. I am particularly anxious, however, that you should get a grip of the subject, for it must be borne in mind that a good boiler is the first essential to a good locomotive.

The steam in the boiler may be likened to the breath in a boy's body. If he wants to run fast and keep it up, he must have plenty of breath. So the fast running express engines must have plenty of steam, and high pressure engines are not much use unless steam can be maintained at high pressure. Boilers are now, of course, very much larger than in the early days, and have enormously increased heating surfaces.

CHAPTER THE TENTH

FUEL AND WATER

EARLY Acts of Parliament authorising the construction of railways all contained a clause to the effect that locomotives should "consume their own smoke," and this accounts for the fact that in the early days of railways the engines used coke fuel, for coke, as perhaps you know, can be burned without the emission of smoke. You may have noticed how clear and bright the coke fires used by night watchmen in the roads burn, and that these fires are practically smokeless.

In the first railway locomotives the combustion of coal was so imperfect that dense clouds of smoke were emitted, and this was forbidden by Parliament. As a result, coke ovens were installed on the railways, and one of these was near West Drayton, the coal being brought by sea from Newcastle to London by small sailing vessels, discharged into barges and hauled up the Grand Junction Canal to West Drayton, where it was converted into coke for the G.W.R. locomotives.

With improvements in the construction of locomotives,

particularly the introduction of the fire-brick arch, and more experience of fuel combustion, it was possible to use coal fuel without creating a smoke nuisance, although full success was not achieved until some twenty years after the opening of the chief main lines of railway.

Coal, as you have no doubt been told at school, is a fossil of vegetable origin principally composed of carbon. Most of the heat produced from coal is obtained by the combustion of the carbon it contains. When carbon burns it combines with oxygen from the air.

Now coal is capable of burning in two ways, or rather the oxygen in the air may combine with the carbon in the coal in two ways, depending on the supply of oxygen. If the air is insufficient for complete combustion, each atom of carbon will combine with one of oxygen to form an inflammable gas, carbon monoxide (CO). Should the supply of each be sufficient, each atom of carbon will combine with two of oxygen, forming a non-inflammable gas, carbon dioxide (CO_2)—your old friend of the chemical "lab." which "turns lime-water milky." This is the product of perfect combustion.

I don't want this to develop into a dry lesson in chemistry, but I am anxious that you should appreciate the importance of a plentiful supply of air to the fire-box of the engine through dampers and fire-hole so as to obtain complete combustion of the coal.

When coal is thrown into a fire-box of sufficient temperature, three distinct stages in combustion occur —firstly, the distillation of gases; secondly, if oxygen is present, these gases are consumed and the oxygen in the air combines with hydrogen (or hydro-carbons) present, to form steam; thirdly, the principal constituent, the coke or free carbon, is consumed.

These chemical reactions occur gradually, commencing on the surface of the coal with which the heat is in contact, and penetrating, with the heat, until the whole is incandescent.

Under practically all conditions a supply of air should be admitted through the fire-door in order to ensure complete combustion. As we have seen, standard G.W.R. fire-door design embodies provision for this supply even when closed.

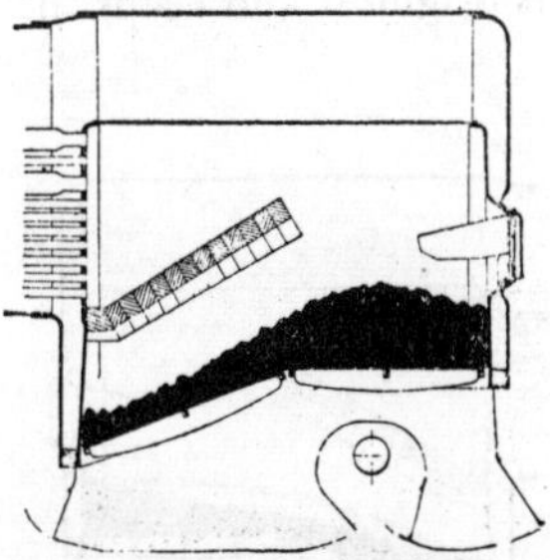

"Middle" Fire

The golden rule for a fireman to observe is to fire "little and often." Dense smoke is a result of indiscriminate firing. Of the many methods of firing—all of which have their advocates—the best known are the middle (or hog's back), flat, saucer, and corner fires.

The first one is made in this way. The fireman spreads the fire already in the fire-box all over the bars evenly, then breaks up lumps of coal to about the size of a cocoanut, and places them evenly over the fire. This is allowed to burn through a little, when more is added in due proportions.

After starting away with the train the fireman loosens the fire in the box by means of the pricker; then at proper intervals he throws on two or three shovelfuls of coal straight in the middle of the fire-box. The small coal remains in the centre and the lumps roll down each side and at the front and back, thus keeping the fire fairly solid in the middle and loose all round. This class of fire is usually employed on the large express engines when on long runs.

A flat fire is started in the same way as the middle fire, but, when running, the fireman simply throws the fresh coal in the places where the fire is brightest and keeps the fire flat all the time.

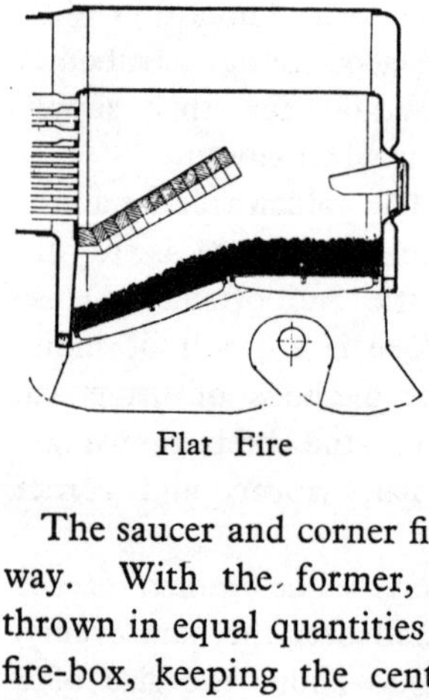

Flat Fire

"Saucer" Fire

The saucer and corner fires are also started in the same way. With the former, when running, fresh coal is thrown in equal quantities all round the four sides of the fire-box, keeping the centre of the box fairly hollow. Hence the term "saucer" fire. With the "corner" fire the fireman places fuel in the four corners only, thus forming four distinct mounds of fire in the box.

The class of fire to be worked depends largely on the quality of the coal supplied, and this is where the art of firing comes in. Careful drivers and firemen make a study of this aspect of their work, and their engines are fired accordingly. There are many kinds of steam coal with varying heating qualities, and it is to the enginemen's advantage to find out which method of firing is best suited to the class of coal on the tender for their use.

So much about food for the locomotive. Now we will have a chat on the drink question.

You are probably familiar with the more common water pillar or water crane from which the tenders or tanks of engines are replenished with water at stations, etc. The old type of pillar tank had a cast iron bottom built up in sections with rust joints and carried on cast iron columns. The newer type, holding 3,000 gallons, has a pressed steel bottom carried on a steel support bolted to a concrete foundation. The feed is regulated by a ball valve.

In some districts the available supply of water is quite unsuitable for use in locomotive boilers, and in order to avoid incrustation of the heating surfaces, etc., many water-softening plants have been installed. The object of these plants is to remove the salts, which cause the "fur," before the water is used in the boilers.

Hard water is water carrying in solution salts, principally of lime and magnesia, as bicarbonates, or sulphates, or both. When hard water is boiled, the dissolved carbon dioxide (which is the solvent for the calcium and magnesium carbonates) is removed, resulting in the precipitation of the calcium carbonate and magnesium hydrate in the boiler.

The presence of the bicarbonates constituting what

is termed the " temporary hardness " (or hardness which can be removed by boiling) is nullified by rendering them insoluble by the addition of lime, which combines with the solvent carbon dioxide, insoluble calcium carbonate and magnesium hydrate being precipitated.

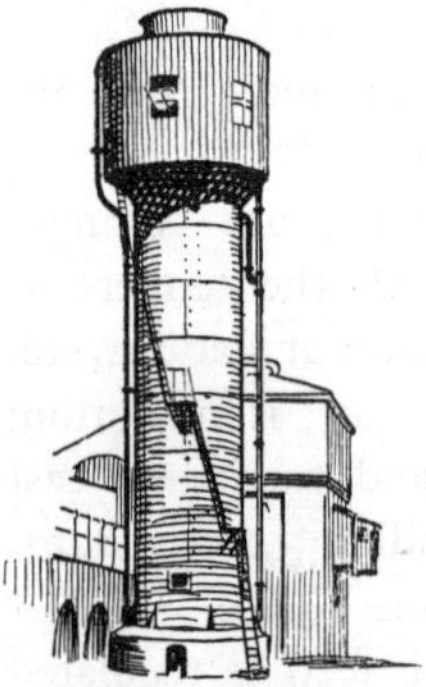

Water Softener

The presence of the sulphates constituting the " permanent hardness " (or hardness that cannot be removed by boiling at atmospheric pressure) is nullified by adding carbonate of soda. The sulphates of lime and magnesia are decomposed and insoluble calcium carbonate and magnesium hydrate formed and precipitated.

I am sorry this is so reminiscent of your chemistry lessons, but you have the advantage that there are no formulæ to remember.

The principles of the various water-softening systems in use are very similar, the plants varying chiefly in lay-out, capacity, and mechanical details.

Tests of the softened water shewing the efficiency of the operations are made daily by the local staff and periodically by chemists from the Swindon Laboratory.

Upwards of one and a half million gallons of water for locomotive purposes are treated by water-softening plants daily on the Great Western Railway.

On our trip to the West you were told about the apparatus which enables engines to pick up water when running at speed. Experiments in this direction were first made in 1895 near Goring, and we shall pass the existing installation there on our way to and from Swindon. The success of these experiments led to many further installations being provided in other parts of the railway, which have been entirely satisfactory.

All modern G.W.R. tender engines are fitted with water scoops, by means of which water is " picked up " on the road; and you will remember troughs are laid

Picking up Water at Goring Water Troughs

in the four-foot way, or, to make it quite clear, between the running rails. These troughs, which are 18 in. wide and 6 in. deep, extend for about a quarter of a mile and are about 50 to 60 miles apart. They are kept full of water by means of a regulating valve, connected from a storage tank through carrying pipes, to the troughs. The water is pumped into the storage tanks by pumps erected near the troughs.

The water scoop is connected at the bottom of an iron

pipe (leading to and from the inside of the tank or tender) by means of a hinge arrangement, the normal position of which is up against the bottom of the tender. A rod is connected with the scoop at one end, and at the other it is coupled to a crank which is actuated by a screw that can be worked from the foot-plate.

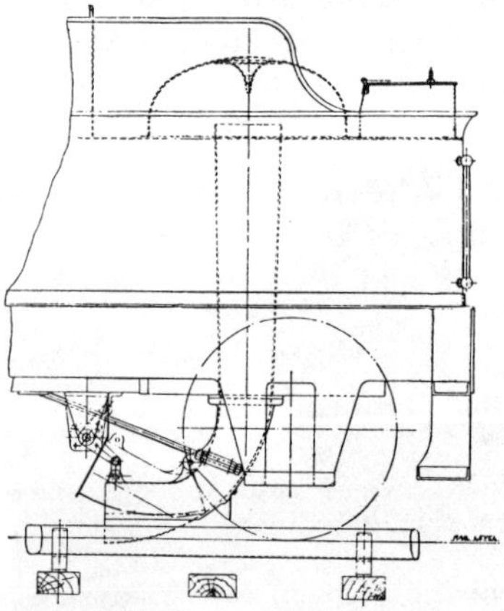

Water Scoop on Locomotive Tender

You may have noticed that there are two, or what appear to be two, brake handles on the tenders. Only the left one acts in this capacity; the right one is the water scoop handle. On reaching the trough where water is to be taken, the fireman unlocks the handle and turns it round; this allows the scoop to be lowered into the trough, and the water is forced by the speed of the train up through the pipe into the tender.

A float indicator is provided on the tender to register how much water is taken in, and the fireman, watching this indicator, screws the scoop up in time to prevent the tender from overfilling.

CHAPTER THE ELEVENTH

HOW THE LOCOMOTIVE WORKS

THE locomotive is a mechanical device for the conversion of heat into work. Heat, in this case, is generated by the combustion of coal or other fuel, in the fire-box of the boiler, and is transferred by conduction to water contained in the body of the boiler, thus producing steam, the medium for storing and conveying the heat to the cylinders of the locomotive, in which it is transformed into work.

If I may say so, you were given a short, but fairly explicit, account of the operation of the locomotive on a former occasion ; but, as we are considering the locomotive to-day, we ought perhaps to have a little chat on " how it works." This is a subject which, if dealt with in any detail, would occupy many hours, but, as you do not want to be here " till the cows come home," I intend to be as brief as possible. Let us refresh our memories.

As the principal component parts of the engine and boiler have already been described, I will now confine myself strictly to the working of the locomotive. Perhaps, meanwhile, you would like to take another look at the

4-6-0 (TWO CYLINDER) EXPRESS PASSENGER LOCOMOTIVE

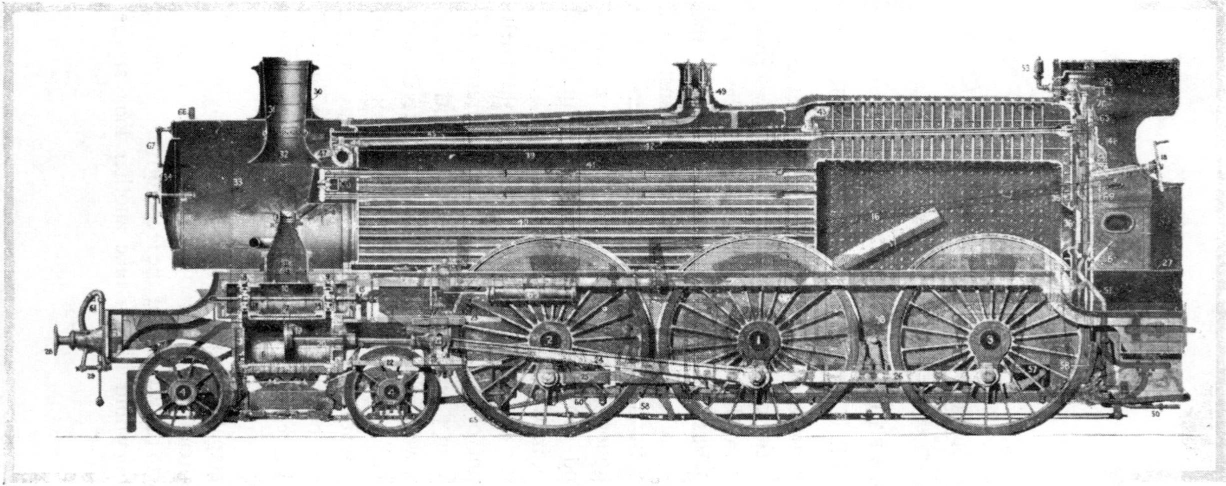

1—Driving Wheel
2—Leading Coupled Wheel
3—Trailing Coupled Wheel
4—Bogie Wheels
5—Life Guard
6—Cylinder
7—Steam Chest
8—Front Steam Port
9—Back Steam Port
10—Live Steam Space
11—Live Steam Admission Passage
12—Blast Pipe
13, 14—Piston Valves
15—Valve Spindle
16—Reversing Rod
17—Reversing Gear in Cab
18—Reversing Gear Handle
19—Piston
20—Piston Rod
21—Crosshead
22 23 Slide Bars
24—Connecting Rod
25—Coupling Rod Leading
26—Coupling Rod Trailing
27—Footplate
28—Buffer
29—Screw Coupling
30—Chimney
31—Chimney (internal)
32—Chimney Bell
33—Smoke Box
34—Smoke Box Door
35—Firebox Water Space
36—Fire Door
37—Brick Arch
38—Fire Bars
39—Boiler Barrel
40—Flue Pipes
41—Superheater Flue Pipes
42—Main Steam Pipe
43—Steam Collecting Mouth
44—Regulator Valve
45—Regulator Rod
46—Regulator Handle
47—Steam Pipe to Superheater
48—Superheater Header
49—Safety Valve
50—Live Steam Injector. Steam Water Connection
51—Live Steam Injector. Steam Pipes
52—Injector Steam Valves
53—Whistles
54—Water Gauge
55—Sight Feed Lubricator
56—Cylinder Cock Handle
57—Ashpan
58—Brake Blocks
59—Brake Pull Rods
60—Vacuum Train Pipe
61—Vacuum Train Pipe Coupling
62—Main Vacuum Reservoir
63—Vacuum Ejector
64—Vacuum Brake Pump
65—Sand Pipe
66—Lamp Iron
67—Hand Rail
68—Whistle Handle
69—Fire Hole Door Handle
70—Handle for closing Water Gauge

By courtesy of the Locomotive Publishing Company

locomotive chart, steam-chest diagram, and photograph of the motion which you were shewn before.

The combustion of fuel, generally coal, in the fire-box of a large boiler generates heat which is transferred to water contained in the enclosed body of the boiler, forming steam under pressure and consequently of very high temperature.

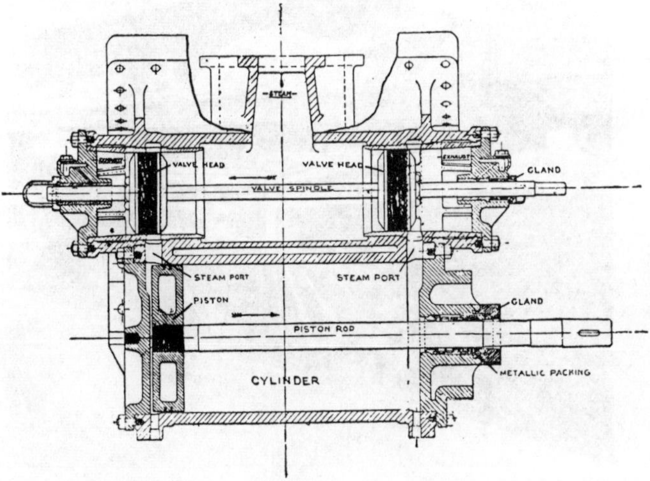

A regulator valve situated in a casting bolted on to the front of the boiler, i.e. in the smoke-box, and operated from the back end by a rod through the boiler, controls the amount of steam passing through the superheater (where the steam is reheated), into the steam-chests and cylinders.

In the steam-chests are valves which distribute and release the steam to and from the cylinders, causing a piston in each to move to and fro.

Attached to each piston is a rod which passes through the back cover of the cylinder, and to which is secured a crosshead sliding between two guide bars.

The piston, rod, and crosshead are therefore moved to and fro by the steam in the cylinders, and this re-

ciprocating motion is converted into the rotary at the wheel by a connecting rod from a pin passing through the crosshead to a pin secured in the wheel a short distance from the axle centre. It will be obvious that twice this distance is the travel or stroke of the piston.

In order to secure four power impulses to a revolution, the pins or cranks of the right- and left-hand engines of the two- and four-cylinder locomotives are set ninety degrees apart.

Steam is only admitted into the cylinders for a certain period of the piston stroke, depending upon the position of the valve gear, which actuates the valves from the movements of the driving axle and the crossheads.

After steam admission to the cylinder is cut off by the valve, the steam, by working expansively, continues to exert a gradually decreasing pressure on the piston until the valve reopens the port, this time to exhaust.

From the cylinders the exhaust steam passes through the blast pipe in the smoke-box and through the chimney to the atmosphere.

Without a lengthy and rather technical description, I do not think much more can be said to amplify the explanation of the working of the " link motion " or reversing gear given on the occasion of " The 10-30 Limited " journey.

This, then, is a short, but I hope clear, statement of " how the locomotive works."

CHAPTER THE TWELFTH

THE ENGINE SHED

THE engine shed may be regarded as the stable or garage for the locomotive, where she receives "grooming" and other attentions between her train duties. Engine sheds are generally of either the "straight road" or turn-table type. The former is one in which a number of parallel short roads

Interior of Straight Road Engine Shed

are laid through the building, and the latter contains one or more turn-tables from which radiate roads of various lengths, one or two from each table leading outside the shed, whilst at least one road connects the tables within the shed.

In each case suitable pits are arranged between the metals, so that men can work beneath the engines when necessary. Smoke troughs are built in the roofs to ensure that, in whatever position an engine is standing, smoke from the chimney will be carried away. Numerous hydrants are fixed between the roads, and adequate lighting is provided.

The shed buildings include suitable offices for foremen and clerical staff, a well-equipped stores, a furnace for drying sand, and mess rooms, with kitchens attached, for the enginemen, firemen, and cleaners.

Besides the staff mentioned, there are employed at the engine shed fire cleaners, lighters up, and call boys. The last-named are employed to carry messages, and call the drivers and firemen during the night hours for the early trains.

A fitting shop is provided, and the larger sheds are also equipped with coppersmiths', blacksmiths', machine and lifting shops. Outside the shed are situated the engine coaling and watering plants, the former consisting of a large coaling stage and the latter of suitable water columns or " cranes."

A coal stage is a means of conveniently handling the coal during its transference from coal wagons to the tenders of engines. It consists of an elevated platform about 13 ft. above the rail level of a road running alongside. On the other side of the stage is an elevated road rising from rail level to within one foot of the platform level, and laid more or less parallel with the stage road. Beyond the stage this elevated road rises on a gradient of 1 in 80, so that wagons shunted to the top can be lowered by gravity to the stage as required. Coal from the wagons is shovelled into trolleys, each of which holds 5 or 10 cwt.; from these it can easily be

Interior of Turn-table Engine Shed

tipped from the side of the platform on to the tenders of engines standing on the coal stage road below.

Special balanced tip platforms are fitted, which normally assume a vertical position. When a trolley is pushed against one of these platforms it tilts outwards over the road until the weight of the trolley forces it to the horizontal position. The trolleys are run between guide rails secured to these platforms, the ends of the rails being turned up so as to form semicircular buffers.

On the top of the coal stage building is situated a

tank (or tanks) of considerable capacity, which form the reservoir for the water supply for the engine shed.

The hard nature of the water generally available for locomotive purposes results in deposits of non-conducting " fur " on the heating surfaces of the boilers,

Coal Stage and Water Column

and to maintain clean boilers frequent washing-out is necessary. All important engine sheds on the Great Western Railway are equipped with hot water boiler washing plant, of which there are two types in use—the overhead and the trough systems respectively.

The overhead system is the one most frequently adopted. It embraces a two-inch overhead steam-pipe, about 14 ft. from the ground, suspended from the roof principals. Vertical down pipes are joined to short lengths of the overhead pipe, forming " T's " each directly over a hydrant. To the ends of these down pipes (about 8 ft. from ground level) steam valves are attached. A stationary boiler, situated in or near the shed supplies steam to the down pipes via the overhead pipes.

When boiler washers use the plant they first remove the cover of an adjacent hydrant and screw on to the hydrant valve a stand pipe 15 in. high, at the top of which is attached a horizontal plug type injector. Connections are now made between the down pipe steam valve and the injector, and to the delivery end of the latter a length of armoured hose is attached, to which detachable nozzles can be fitted. The hydrant and steam valves are then opened with the injector lever in the "shut" position. By placing the lever in the "open" position the resulting jet of hot water through the nozzle is about 120° F., and has a throw of 60 ft. The quantity of water passing would be about 40 gallons a minute, and this hot water at high pressure is used for the periodical washing out of the engine boilers, as I will explain a little later.

We will now follow a locomotive which has arrived at shed, the driver and fireman having booked off duty. The locomotive is stopped in a road conveniently near the coal stage.

The shed turner, or in some cases a pilotman, then assumes responsibility for the engine, which he takes on to the coal stage road. There, whilst waiting in turn for coal, the smoke-box ashes are shovelled out and dumped alongside, or, as in the case of the Old Oak Common

(London) Shed, removed by a special pneumatic ejector direct into a truck.

The engine is then moved forward and stopped under the coal stage tip, from which coal is dumped into the tender in the manner already described.

The quality and quantity of the coal supplied to an engine depend upon the nature and mileage of its next turn, and of this the shed turner is advised by the foreman. Circumstances sometimes necessitate the mixing of coals of different qualities, this being carried out by the coal stage men, who distribute the coal available to the best advantage.

After coaling, the engine is taken over a "fire-dropping" pit, where the fire is either cleaned or dropped, according to the period elapsing before it is again required in service. When a fire is cleaned a fire-dropper, standing on the foot-plate, shovels out through the fire-hole all the clinker and dirt in the fire by means of a long-handled shovel. The clinker is dumped alongside between the pits, cooled with water from a hose pipe, and finally removed, as are also the ashes raked out from the ash-pan into the pit. After fire-cleaning, a low fire is maintained until the engine is again required in traffic.

The dropping of a fire is a similar operation, but in this case, in addition to the removal of the clinker and dirt, all the unconsumed portion of the fire is shovelled out. This is done when the boiler has to be allowed to cool down before the next trip.

After fire-dropping, and whilst the boiler is still in steam, the tubes are "blown" or cleaned. This operation is performed as follows: Any deposits at the fire-box end of the tubes are swept off with a wire brush, and the tip of a steam lance of steel pipe, mounted upon a similar handle to that of a spade, is inserted in the smoke-box end of each tube in turn. The back end of the lance is connected by a flexible armoured pipe to a suitable steam valve screwed

Fire-dropping

into the smoke-box front plate and connected direct to the boiler. When this cock is open, and a convenient secondary control (operated by the man's knee) also opened, a jet of steam passes through the tube with a velocity sufficient to remove all excessive deposits of soot, etc., therein. Should any of the tubes be completely blocked they are "run" with a "screw-driver" rod, which consists of a long rod, through an eye in the end of which is threaded a bunch of trimming wire. When this operation is completed the engine is taken to the shed and placed over a pit.

The fitters or boiler smiths, who have been duly

notified of any defects, can now rectify the troubles. These defects are of several kinds. A cock may be leaking, piston rod packing may need attention, brakes require adjusting, etc.

Possibly the engine is due for one of the following periodical examinations :

Smoke-boxes, water gauges, vacuum brake gear, and pressure gauge – – – –	Examined monthly
Safety valves – – – –	Examined yearly
Boiler (by Shed Staff) – –	Examined monthly
Boiler (by Running Department Inspector) – – – –	Examined half-yearly
Piston and valves, Express engines	After 20,000 miles
„ „ „ Freight „	„ 15,000 „
„ „ „ Shunting „	„ 12,000 „

If this is the case, it is "stopped"—that is, taken out of traffic until the examination and any subsequent repairs are completed. Boilers are generally washed out weekly with hot water, the operation taking a "set" of boiler washers, comprising two men, from three to five hours, according to the size and state of the boiler.

To wash out a boiler all plugs and mud hole doors are removed, and while one man operates the injector, his mate inserts a nozzle into each plug hole in systematic rotation. The hot water under high pressure and the vigorous working of rods over the surfaces, loosens the "fur," which is afterwards swilled out of the mud holes. The nozzles used are of various shapes, and a suitable one is attached to the hosepipe for each plug hole.

After a thorough scouring the boiler is inspected internally by a boilersmith with an acetylene light and small adjustable mirror. The lamp used is worthy of mention. It comprises a small generator connected to a jet by a long flexible pipe. The jet is secured to the end of a steel rod, $\frac{1}{8}$ in. diameter and 4 ft. long, in such a manner that the face of the jet is protected by the end of the rod. This is a most convenient form of lamp for the purpose, enabling the inspector to insert the flame through the plug and mud holes well into the boiler whilst leaving the generator safely on any convenient fitting.

After the boiler is certified " clean and in good order," all the mud hole door joints are made and the doors secured. The plugs are also inserted and tightened (with the exception of one top plug) having previously been well lubricated with graphite grease.

The boiler is then filled through the remaining plug hole up to the " half glass " level, when the plug is inserted and screwed down.

Several cleaners now take charge of the engine, and by scouring thoroughly with special oil and water, with the aid, when necessary, of a slab of bath-brick, remove dirt from all accessible parts. After this a coat of petroleum jelly is generally applied to all the paint-work and polished steel surfaces, such as the coupling and connecting rods, etc.

A " lighter-up " acquainted with the turns of the engines lights the fires in rotation, allowing a period of five hours for a large boiler and three hours for a small boiler, in which to raise steam in readiness for the road at the booked time.

As may be imagined, lighting a fire in the large grate of a modern locomotive is not a simple undertaking, and must be carried out methodically. In order to facilitate rapid lighting up, and promote economy in initial fuel consumption, bundles of wood are prepared, as in this photograph, at the larger sheds and distributed throughout the division. The "lighter-up" covers the larger part of the grate with coal, leaving only a small area uncovered in the centre of the back end conveniently near the fire-hole. This is done to concentrate the subsequent current of air through a small area of the grate.

To the front end of this uncovered portion he throws a large piece of coal, which later prevents the scattering of the ignited part of the fire. Then a piece of dirty and well-oiled waste (discarded by the cleaners) is ignited from a portable paraffin lamp and thrown on to the bars, followed by one or two bundles of wood (according to the size of the grate). Pieces of coal are next judiciously added, and the fire is fostered by the fire-lighter's mate until the whole body of fuel is well alight.

Our locomotive has now had her "wash and brush up," and is spick and span and ready for another trip.

CHAPTER THE THIRTEENTH

THE ENGINE CREW

THE finest locomotive would be of little use without a trained crew to control it, and lack of efficiency in the driver or fireman might soon spell ruin to the best engine in the world.

As nearly every boy at some time or another passes through the period when he longs to grow up quickly and become an engine-driver, I am sure you will be interested in having a few details of the duties of the engine crew.

Engine-drivers do not enter the railway service as such, but have to work their way up gradually from engine cleaners, through the grades of shunting firemen, local goods firemen and main line firemen, finishing as firemen on express passenger trains.

Before being graded as engine-drivers and allowed to take charge of an engine, firemen have to pass a severe examination as to their knowledge of the engine generally, and how to deal with minor failures of the various parts. Preparation for this examination involves a good deal of hard work and study. For their assistance in this respect "Mutual Improvement Classes" are established at practically all Locomotive Depôts, and the drivers, firemen, and cleaners meet at least once a week to discuss and study the various parts of the engine.

When booking on duty the driver has first of all to examine the notice boards for particulars of any signal alterations, permanent way restrictions, or other matters affecting the section of the line over which he has to run. He then draws from the stores the oil, cotton waste, and other material required for the day. He must satisfy himself that the requisite amount of coal is on his tender, examine springs, test set bolts, etc., inspect trimmings (lubricating), and oil the various working parts of his engine.

At the booked time, the driver leaves the shed with his engine for the station. After the engine has been coupled to the train, the driver tests his vacuum brake by means of the steam ejector. He then ascertains from the guard the number of vehicles on the train and other particulars regarding the trip they are about to make.

The high speeds and punctuality of trains obtaining on the Great Western Railway necessitate a thorough knowledge of the road, and a close study of official instructions by both driver and fireman. Many temporary speed restrictions and signal checks are encountered in addition to permanent way restrictions, and all these have to be complied with immediately, requiring a keen look out by the engine crew throughout the run.

The driver must be well acquainted with the booked timing of the train (this is obtained from the time service books), so that he may pass, or stop, at the proper booked times. The working time-table differs very much from the time-table issued to the public, and besides giving time of arrival and departure for all places at which a train stops, it also gives the times at which the train is due to pass certain stations, junctions, signal boxes, etc.

On starting away, and all the time his train is in motion, the driver must observe the many signals on the road, be on the look out for persons or cattle straying on the permanent way, or any other obstructions. He must sound his whistle at certain crossings, and also at certain signal boxes, in order to advise the signalman of the route he is booked to travel over.

The driver must see that the fireman maintains ample steam pressure and keeps up the supply of water in the boiler, that the coal is being used properly, and also that there is not too much fire in the fire-box at the end of the journey, which would, of course, mean waste of fuel.

On leaving the train and taking his engine to shed, the driver examines it carefully to see if there are any defects. Such matters have to be reported in a book provided for the purpose. The driver then makes out his log on the proper form, hands it in at the office, and books off duty.

Among some delightful verses for children included in " A Little of Everything," Mr. E. V. Lucas says of the engine-driver :

The Driver's a man of the worthiest type,
Who leans on the engine and smokes his pipe,
Or sends her along, if he feels inclined,
Twice as fast as the fastest wind ;
Who sits by the fire if it rains or freezes,
And blows the whistle whenever he pleases.

Few will dispute the truth of the first line, and we will be charitable enough to assume that the second refers to the driver's off-duty hours. The speed suggestion is worthy of the Great Western Railway, and the writer was evidently looking into the future (the verses were written some years ago) and foresaw the provision of seats for the men in the engine cab, which are a feature of the more modern types of Great Western locomotives.

Now for the fireman : let us see just what his duties are. From what you already know about coal consumption you will realise that to be fireman on one of the modern express engines is not exactly a rest cure.

After booking on duty and obtaining from the office the keys of the tool-boxes, the fireman puts out the various tools required for the trip. The water-gauge is then tested to see that it works properly, the fire-box examined, and the fire (which has already been lighted and should be burning satisfactorily) made up by placing small lumps of coal evenly over the bars. He then examines the smoke-box, screws the door up tightly, and inspects the sand-boxes to see that they contain a sufficient supply of dry sand. It is also his duty to see that the ash-pan is properly cleaned out, and that the tank or tender is full of water. He must also satisfy himself that the head and gauge lamps are properly trimmed and that the cases are clean. On coupling up to the train, the head lamps are arranged in accordance with the code which indicates the class of train, i.e. whether express passenger, slow goods, live stock, etc.

The fireman's principal duty is to maintain a boiler pressure suitable to the varying conditions of working, and to obtain the utmost heat from the coal. This he does by firing to suit the individual boiler and the conditions prevailing, and endeavouring by regulating the supply of air through dampers and fire-hole door to the fire-box, to obtain complete combustion of the fuel.

In addition he replenishes the boiler with water by operating the injectors. Two injectors are usually fitted; both can use live steam from the boiler, but one injector also utilises exhaust steam from the cylinders when running. Water levels in boiler and tanks are ascertained by reference to a gauge glass and graduated indicator respectively.

The fireman's duties also include working the hand brake and the water picking up apparatus for replenishing the tanks. The latter involves lowering, by means of a hand screw, a scoop situated under the tender, when running over water-troughs. If the engine is not fitted with a scoop, the fireman has to take water by means of the columns provided at certain stations where the train is booked to stop.

During the run the fireman regulates the fire and the water level in the boiler, so that at stations where the train is booked to stop there shall be no blowing off at the safety valves, which, besides being wasteful, is a nuisance owing to the noise.

At the end of the journey and on arrival at the shed, the fireman has to clean and lock up all the tools, lamps, etc.. in readiness for the next day's trip.

Mr. Lucas, in the verses already referred to, has also a few lines about the fireman or "stoker," as he terms him:

The Stoker stands by the engine fire,
And feeds the flames to their full desire;
At night he opens the furnace door,
And the train tears by with a glare and a roar;
He oils the engine from time to time,
And covers himself with grease and grime,
Then cleans his hands in an absent way
On a piece of rag as dirty as they.
An engine stoker I'd like to be,
Except for the trouble of washing for tea.

From which you see that even the most fascinating occupations are not without their disadvantages. I would hardly like to say that a fireman can keep as clean at his work as, say, a shop-walker, but with modern methods of lubrication, etc., it is not necessary for him to convert himself into an Ethiopian exactly.

Drivers and firemen are divided up into what are termed "links," according to the class of engine, the different trains to be worked, and also the seniority of the men. The senior drivers and firemen as a rule work the express passenger trains with the large express engines, and a link is formed of a sufficient number of men and engines to cope with the number of express trains to be run.

As an example, we will suppose that during the twenty-four hours there are ten express trains to be provided for. To meet this demand, a link of twelve drivers and an equal number of firemen is formed to work round in rotation on these trains. Each set (or pair) of men must have twelve hours off duty between each turn of duty, so it is obvious that men working to-day on the last late turn cannot work the first early turn to-morrow. Hence the appointment of more men than there are turns of duty to enable one or two sets, as the case may be, to have an "off duty" day, after which they can start again on the early turn the day after being off duty.

This principle is followed all down the scale for the various classes of engines from express passenger train links to the shunting engine links.

"Yes," you say, "but what about special trains which are ordered out at short notice?" Well, to cope with any special work that may crop up, certain men are put in a special link. These are the handy men who are well acquainted with the various sections of the railway to which their depôt applies.

CHAPTER THE FOURTEENTH

LOCOMOTIVE RUNNING TESTS

APART from the testing of locomotives under everyday running conditions, the actual working of the engines is also investigated with greater thoroughness and on more scientific lines by means of stationary test plant and by the dynamometer car. We hope to inspect the stationary testing plant at Swindon, and you will then be told something of its functions.

A modern dynamometer car enables the most searching tests to be made and records to be taken almost continuously on a long run under varying conditions of actual working, and important data, such as the drawbar pull, speed and acceleration, superheater and smoke-box temperatures and a number of other important factors, can be ascertained with absolute accuracy.

The dynamometer car used on the Great Western Railway, designed and built in the Swindon Works, is 48 ft. 5 in. long over buffers and weighs 27 tons 3 cwt. It is carried on two 4-wheeled bogies, and has an extra wheel for driving the apparatus. The body is divided into three compartments, the largest, containing the recording instruments, being 27 ft. 3 in. long, with a maximum width of 8 ft. 6 in. inside—that is, around the instrument table—thus affording added space for moving about and enabling a better look-out to be obtained. Behind the instrument compartment is another containing a cupboard for stores, tool lockers, and a battery of secondary cells for the electrically-operated instruments. As already stated, the gear is actuated by means of an extra wheel, which can be raised or lowered into contact with the rail as required. This wheel is only lowered when a test is actually being made. It is fitted with a hardened steel tyre accurately ground to such a diameter as to make exactly 440 revolutions per mile run. The apparatus with which the car is equipped provides for the taking of various measurements and records.

[By Courtesy of *Railway Gazette*

Instruments in Dynamometer Car

One of the "Castle" class engines, No. 4074, "Caldicot Castle," has recently been undergoing such tests between Swindon and Plymouth, and by this means most valuable information as to the performance of this class of engine has been ascertained. For these trials certain additional apparatus was fitted. Three sets of trials were made on special trains running from Swindon to Plymouth (North Road) and back. You will like to hear something about these tests.

[By Courtesy of *Railway Gazette*

" Caldicot Castle " equipped for Running Tests

The load on the down trips consisted of fourteen heavy 70-ft. eight-wheeled coaches and the dynamometer car from Swindon to Taunton, eleven coaches and the car from Taunton to Newton Abbot, and eight coaches and the car from Newton Abbot to Plymouth. On the up trips the load was eight coaches and the car from Plymouth to Newton Abbot, and fourteen coaches and the car thence to Swindon. The trains were timed so as to run, at any part of the journey, at a speed equal to the fastest expresses running over that part of the railway.

Measurements and records were made of:

1. Indicated horse-power.
2. Pressure in the steam-chest.
3. Drawbar pull and drawbar horse-power.
4. Speed.
5. Steam pressure, cut off, opening of regulator, and height of water in gauge-glass.
6. Coal consumed.
7. Water consumed.
8. Oil consumed.
9. Vacuum in the smoke-box and pressure in the ash-pan.
10. Temperature of the feed water in the tender.
11. Temperature of the feed water entering the boiler.
12. Pressure of the exhaust steam entering the exhaust steam injector.
13. Temperature of: (*a*) Superheater flues; (*b*) Steam entering the superheater; (*c*) Steam leaving the superheater; (*d*) Steam entering the steam-chest; (*e*) Smoke-box generally.
14. The chemical composition of: (*a*) Smoke-box gases; (*b*) Coal (also the calorific value); (*c*) Smoke-box ashes; (*d*) Ashes in the ash-pan.
15. Weight of the smoke-box ashes.
16. Weight of the ash-pan ashes.
17. Wind and weather.

To obtain the record of the pull on the drawbar, a special spring is provided underneath the dynamometer car, to which the drawbar at one end—known as the " live " end—is attached. A full description of the apparatus would be rather technical and not a little tedious, so, perhaps, it will suffice to say that attachments to the spring are coupled to a bar running longitudinally with the car and across the instrument table in the car. A stylographic pen is attached to the rod and records deflections of the drawbar on paper as the latter moves over the table.

The work on the drawbar is recorded by an instrument known as an " integrator." The gearing of the apparatus is so arranged that each revolution of a roller represents 330,000 ft. lb. of work. The revolutions are recorded on paper by means of an electromagnetic pen and counted by an electric counter.

To obtain the speed of the train a clock is provided which is in electric connection with an electromagnetic pen. As the paper moves over the instrument table at a rate proportional to that of the train, the speed is accurately ascertained by reading off the records made by a suitably graduated scale.

The indicated horse-power and the steam-chest pressure were measured by means of four indicators, which automatically recorded on cards the data required. Record cards were taken from both cylinders and steam-chests at predetermined spots, the operator in charge of the indicating giving word to those on the indicator, at the same time signalling the taking of the cards to the dynamometer car by pressing an electric push.

The records of steam pressure, cut off, etc., were taken by an observer in the driver's cab, the time at which each change occurred being noted and signalled electrically to the dynamometer car.

In order to measure the coal consumed, the coal space of the tender was increased by the temporary addition of 1 ft. to its height, so that enough coal could be carried to run from Swindon to Plymouth and back. After coaling, the tank was filled to a mark and the tender weighed. On returning to Swindon after each trial the tank was again filled to the same height and the tender re-weighed. The difference in the two weights thus gave the coal burned on the journey.

Only the coal actually burnt in running was determined. The fire was made up before starting with unweighed coal, and the trip was finished with the same amount of coal in the fire-box (as nearly as could be judged) as at the start.

To measure the water consumed a special indicator was fitted to the tender, which was worked from the ordinary indicator float and carefully calibrated by filling the tender through a tested water meter. The record of water used for watering the coal was determined in the following manner. An attachment was made to the coal-watering cock which closed an electric circuit, and so deflected a pen in the dynamometer car whenever the cock was opened. The total time that the cock was opened could thus be determined. A unit was ascertained before the trials by opening the cock for a given time and weighing the water that passed through. The total amount of water used in this way throughout any trip could thus be readily ascertained.

The oil consumed was ascertained by issuing a known quantity to the driver before each trip and measuring what was left at the end of the journey. All oil cups and lubricators were filled with unmeasured oil before the trials and again at the end of each run. Only the oil actually used in running was thus recorded.

The vacuum and pressure in smoke-box and ash-pan, respectively, were recorded by means of instruments known as " U " tube manometers, the record being taken from the centre of both smoke-box and ash-pan. The manometers were fixed on the front of the engine on the left-hand side, and read by an observer. The latter also operated the cocks for smoke-box gas analysis.

The temperature of the feed water in the tender was obtained by drawing samples at intervals and inserting an ordinary mercury thermometer. That of the water entering the boiler was taken by means of a distance thermometer, the bulb being inserted in the delivery pipe.

The pressure of the exhaust steam entering the injector was taken by a pressure gauge specially constructed at Swindon to read low pressures.

The temperatures of smoke-box, superheater, etc., were all taken by means of an apparatus known as a six-station pyrometer. Its operation depends on the fact that, when two dissimilar metals are brought into contact and the ends in contact are hotter than the other ends, a small electromotive force is generated.

By attaching wires to the cold ends and leading them to a suitable meter the difference in temperature between the hot and cold ends can be read. The cold ends in this case were all brought to a box fixed on the front of the engine, and the temperature of this box was read by the observer by means of a mercury thermometer. From the box five coils of wire were led to a switch-board in the dynamometer car, by means of which all of them could be connected in turn to a galvanometer graduated in degrees of temperature. Readings were taken at the same time as the indicator cards. When the operator in charge of the indicating signalled to the dynamometer car the fact of the cards

[By Courtesy of *Railway Gazette*

In the Dynamometer Car. Making Chemical Analysis of Smoke-box Gases

being taken, the pressing of his push, besides deflecting the pen, rang bells on the front of the engine and in the car, thus warning the operator to take readings.

The analysis of the smoke-box gases was made *en route* in the dynamometer car. The gases were collected from points 9 in. from the front of the tube plate, at the levels of the superheater tubes and the bottom row of flue tubes respectively. Pipes passed from these through the special apparatus to the vacuum train-pipe in the driver's cab.

The analysis of the coal and ashes was made by collecting samples at the end of each outward trip, and analysing them in the laboratory at Swindon.

The direction of the wind was taken by means of a vane and the pressure by an anemometer.

The object of all these tests may not be equally apparent to you, but I can assure you they are of the greatest possible value to the locomotive engineers. They are typical of the scientific manner in which modern investigations into locomotive performances are made, as well as of the up-to-date methods obtaining on the Great Western Railway.

And now I think—keen as I know you are on railways—you have had an ample sufficiency of the railway locomotive for one day. To-morrow we will go to Swindon, by the 10.45 A.M. train from Paddington, and make a tour of the locomotive shops, where we should see some of the operations which we have been talking about actually going on. I think I can promise you an interesting day, and we will try and time our departure from the Works so as to travel back from Swindon on the famous 3.45 P.M. train—the fastest in the Kingdom.

Now you can sleep on the prospect. I shall expect to see you just before 10.45 to-morrow morning on No. 2 platform, Paddington Station. Remember Great Western trains leave promptly, and please don't be late!

CHAPTER THE FIFTEENTH

CONSTRUCTING A LOCOMOTIVE

You are sharp on time and our train is just off. As we have already travelled the section Paddington to Reading together on our trip by "The 10.30 Limited," I think we might do worse than employ our time on that portion of our journey this morning with a talk about the construction of a locomotive. You will then be better able to follow the various processes when you see them going on before your eyes in the Swindon shops. I think a few photographs will assist us in this direction.

The initial work in the construction of a locomotive takes place in the Drawing Office. Shop drawings have to be prepared, and when these are approved the various shops are supplied with schedules of parts, giving drawing numbers and quantities, so that they can prepare the necessary patterns, templates, etc., preparatory to castings and forgings being made. You will understand that all the shops supplying locomotive parts have to keep well ahead of the work in the erecting shop, in order that the men may be kept employed and not lose time waiting for fittings.

The pattern shops supply the patterns for steel, iron, gun-metal or brass castings, and the machine shops have to supply templates for the forgings, and also to scheme and make special jigs to enable the workmen to produce the castings and forgings to standard in order to ensure interchangeability. The boiler shop will also require templates for the boiler plates and dies for pressed steel parts.

Besides the work produced at Swindon, a large quantity of steel castings is ordered from the various steel foundries in the country, and patterns have to be supplied to firms undertaking this work. Steel castings are required for wheel centres, pistons, motion plates, bogie centres and a number of other parts, whilst forgings have to be made for connecting rods, coupling rods, eccentric straps, motion bars, valve gear, brake gear, etc. Heavy forgings are made under the steam hammer, while lighter ones are stamped out. The cylinder castings have, of course, to be most accurately bored and faced, the sides planed to fit the frames, and holes drilled for fastening on the cylinder and steam-chest covers, before they are ready for the erecting shop.

The frame plates as received from the steel mills are very different from the finished product, being merely steel plate about 30 ft. long by 4 ft. wide and $1\frac{1}{4}$ in. thick. They are first punched out roughly to the shape of the frame required, a template being used to mark off each plate, then they are annealed in a large furnace and levelled, after which they are ready for machining.

Eight or ten plates, according to the thickness, are stacked one on top of another on the bed of the large slotting machine which you see in this photograph. The top plate is marked off from a template to the finished dimensions, and the whole is slotted to the lines and can then be passed on to a special radial arm drilling machine, where all holes for fastening the cylinders, motion plates,

Frame Slotting Machine

axle box guides, etc., are drilled. The frame plates are then passed on to the erecting shop.

The forgings and castings for the valve gear and motion require a lot of work in the machine shop before they are ready for the erectors. Piston rods are turned direct from the rolled bar. When this has been done they are ready for the head (which has been turned, bored and screwed in a heavy chuck lathe) to be screwed on. After this is done they pass forward to a grinding lathe for finishing.

Piston valves, which are used so largely on Great Western Railway modern engines, require very careful and accurate machining, and there are at Swindon some of the most modern appliances for their manufacture. As we shall see, the heads and rings are bored and turned on a special mandrel to within a few thousandths of an inch of the finished dimensions. The faces are then scraped up by hand, so that the width over each ring and over all is correct when tested with a micrometer. The eccentrics for actuating the valves are of cast iron, and are machined and bored in a chuck lathe ready for keying on the driving axle. The eccentric straps are forged under the steam hammer from mild steel slabs and require machining all over. Cast iron and cast steel straps have been tried, but neither have given such freedom from failure as the forged straps.

The valve rods, connecting rods, and coupling rods are all forged at Swindon from special steel blooms, and are machined all over, careful examination being made to ensure them being absolutely flawless. You will see the large milling machines used for milling them to "I" section at Swindon, which gives a light yet rigid rod.

The brake gear is machined and assembled, but time does not permit of my describing the different processes of manufacture.

Axle boxes are largely steel castings having a bronze lining forced in with a hydraulic press for the bearing. They are planed at the sides to work in the horn cheeks or guides, and the lining is rough cut in a slotting machine about $\frac{3}{8}$ in. larger in diameter than the axle journal that has to run in it. A white metal facing is then cast upon the rough surface of the lining and turned in a lathe to the required diameter. These and other operations are checked carefully with gauges to ensure the box being central and square with the sides.

The cast steel wheel centres received from the steel foundry require the bosses faced and bored before they can be pressed on a turned axle with a hydraulic press. They are then turned, as we shall see, in large double-face plate lathes over the rim, to enable rolled steel tyres to be shrunk on them. The tyres are then turned up to

Built-up Balanced Crank, " Castle Class "

gauges to ensure their being of the correct section and true to gauge. The axles for an outside cylinder engine are straight shafts of mild steel, which will require the journals and the wheel seats turned to size. The journals are finished with a hardened steel roller to compress the skin and give a hard, smooth surface.

If the engine has inside cylinders, crank axles are built up with slabs for the webs and rolled bar for the shaft, or else expensive steel forgings are purchased. The present practice is to build up the crank shafts, and experience certainly proves it to be the best. The slabs from which the webs are made for the built-up cranks are planed to gauge size for width and thickness, and are then placed in a special turn-table jig under a special boring mill.

A " cheese " is cut out of each end of the slab, and the jig is made so that the holes have the correct distance between the centres for the throw of the crank. Holes are then bored out to the finished size, ready to be shrunk on to pieces of turned shaft which have been prepared, after which two steel keys are screwed in. When the crank is complete it is put in one of the special crank lathes, and the shafts and crank pins are trued to finished sizes. Forged cranks are roughed out on special machines and finished in the same way. Key ways are now milled and the wheels keyed on ready for turning.

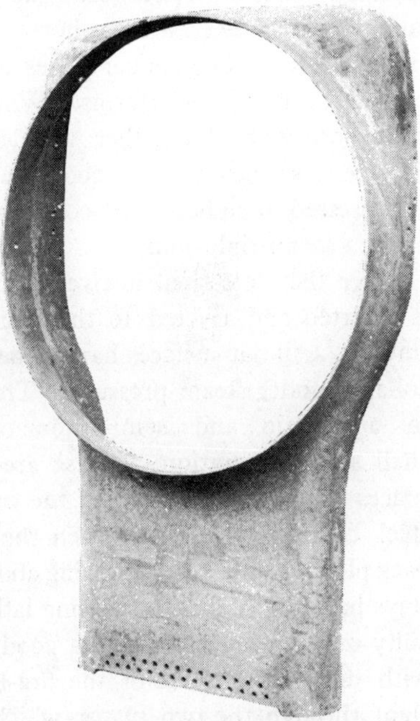

Copper Throat Plate

Now we come to the boiler. Great Western Railway practice is to construct the outside fire-box casing and barrel of mild steel sheets, and the inside fire-box of copper plates. The barrel plates are first levelled to remove any buckles in them, and then rolled to the correct diameter. If they are for the cone-shaped barrel, they require a considerable amount of care in the marking off and rolling. The throat and tube plates are pressed from flat plate in a large hydraulic press which we shall see in operation. Afterwards the flanges are cut to the right dimensions in a large horizontal band saw or with circular saws. The copper plates are flanged with wooden mallets over cast iron forms. Whenever possible, boiler plates are riveted together with hydraulic riveters, not only because the rivets are good, but the plates themselves are pressed together very considerably, which helps to make a steam-tight joint.

After the steel shell is riveted up, the copper fire-box is inserted and riveted to the foundation ring ready for staying. All flat surfaces have to be stayed, or they would collapse under steam pressure. The steel stays are made in automatic and semi-automatic lathes, which we shall see in operation. These are for staying the wide spaces between the crown of the copper fire-box and the steel casing, and also between the front tube plate and back plate and the sides of casing above the crown. Copper stays have to be made in chasing lathes, owing to the difficulty experienced in cutting a good thread on copper bar with dies. The sides of the fire-box have holes drilled right through the two plates, which are tapped ready for copper stays to be screwed in. As you will see, compressed air plays a very important part in these operations, holes being drilled and tapped by its aid in places where it would be impossible to do it on large drilling machines. It is also used for riveting the stay heads over, and for chipping and caulking the seams, as well as for boiler repairs. Compressed air is used to a limited extent for riveting, but is not so satisfactory as hydraulic power.

After the barrel is riveted up to the fire-box casing, the tubes are inserted in the front and back tube plates,

Tapping Stay Holes in Fire-box by Compressed Air

expanded, and beaded with roller expanders driven by a small air drill. The boiler is now ready for the seatings of the safety valves, regulator-box, water-gauge frame, ejector, etc., which are all bedded on to the steel plate, riveted, and caulked to make a permanent steam-tight job. After this, the boiler is ready for testing—first, hydraulically, by filling it full of water, blanking up all holes, and, by means of a wood fire, expanding the water to a test pressure, taking care that it does not rise above about 120° F. If this is satisfactory, the boiler is tested under steam for six hours, and then passed on to the erecting shop.

No. 7 Standard Boiler

So much for locomotive construction, or, rather, the construction of locomotive parts. We will now have a few words about the erecting of a locomotive, or assembly of its various parts.

CHAPTER THE SIXTEENTH

ERECTING A LOCOMOTIVE

We will assume that all the main parts have arrived at the erecting shop and we can now watch the fascinating process of erection. Here are some photographs shewing a tank engine in the various stages of erection which will help you to follow my story.

The frames are placed on low trestles, the centre lines of the axles are marked off, and horn blocks or cheeks are fitted into place. The holes, already drilled in the frames, are marked off on the flanges of the horn cheeks, and these are sent to a machine for drilling. The brackets for carrying the foot-plate and outside frame are also marked off, drilled and riveted on. The frames are now mounted on stands and set parallel and square. The cylinders are then put on the frames, centre lines of whipcord are passed through the cylinders to a straight edge, and measurements taken from the cord to the edge of the horn

Laying down Frames

Setting up Cylinders

cheeks. When these measurements are equal, the cylinders are in the correct carrying position and the holes can be drilled for bolting them to the frames, turned bolts being driven in. Expansion stays and boiler carrying brackets are positioned, marked off, drilled and riveted up.

The axle boxes are next fitted up between the horn cheeks so that they can be moved up and down freely. After being fitted in the horns they are bedded on the axle journals. The boiler can now be put in position, the fire-box passing between the frames until the carrying brackets, which are studded to the boiler, rest on top of the frames, and the smoke-box rests in the saddle casting on the cylinders. The boiler is fixed with brackets which are bolted to the frames and clip the carrying brackets on the fire-box. The smoke-box is bolted securely to the saddle casting, but the barrel only rests on the carrying bracket. The motion plates are bolted to an extension of the boiler carrying bracket, and are now put up ready for the motion bars. These are fixed at one end to the back cylinder cover and at the other to the motion plate.

While this work is in hand the boiler and cylinders can be covered with magnesia asbestos (non-heat-conductor) and mild steel plates, and, if it is a tank engine, the tanks can be fitted and fixed and cab plates put up. The piston rings are fitted in the cylinders and put in the grooves of piston heads. They are now put in the cylinders and motion blocks fixed on.

The engine is now lifted and placed on its wheels, connecting rods put up, and valve gear connected up ready for the valve setters. Any adjustment necessary is made, either to the eccentric rods, or the eccentrics, and the

Placing Boiler in position

Fitting Water Tanks

Getting ready for Wheels

On Electric Traverser

engine is ready for trial. While these latter operations have been in progress the brake work has been going up, injectors have been fixed, pipes made and put in position, and the hundred and one smaller fittings have been added. The painters have also been at work putting on the priming coats, white lead stopping, rubbing down,

Engine Ready for the Road

and applying the familiar G.W.R. colours. The lining is now done and the whole varnished, the engine being then ready for the factory trials.

All engines, after completion in the shops, are weighed in working order to adjust the weight on each wheel and to level the frames. An ingenious weighing machine at Swindon simultaneously indicates upon separate dials the weight on each wheel.

After weighing, our engine goes for a short run to try all the gear, and on its return any necessary adjustments are made. It then has another run, and, if satisfactory, it is handed over to the running department at Swindon. Before being sent to the station to which it is allocated, it works a local goods or passenger train for two or three days, so that everything will find its bearing, and any defects that develop may be remedied before the engine leaves Swindon.

And now I see we have arrived at Reading, where we make a short stop. At Reading we take the old main line route for Swindon.

After a five minutes' stop at Reading we are on our way again. From your seat, facing the engine, you see high ground on your right-hand side. This is Caversham Heights, a residential district, at the foot of which lies one of the prettiest reaches of the Thames. We catch a fleeting view of the river as we run through Tilehurst. We now pass the village of Purley and the Mapledurham Woods as we speed on to Pangbourne, a favourite resort of river folk.

We are now over the Goring water-troughs, and you will see on your right the water-softening plant from which the troughs are supplied. At this point we cross the Thames again and get another charming view of the river.

Now we pass Goring and Streatley Station, the twin villages which lie on either bank of the river. Yet again, we cross the Thames near Cholsey and Moulsford, which is the junction station for Wallingford—an old-fashioned riverside town full of historical interest.

Just before reaching Didcot you see in the distance, on the right, two tree-capped hills. These are Wittenham Clumps, a familiar landmark for many miles round.

Didcot is a station of considerable importance from a railway point of view, as from here a line runs northwards via Oxford to Aynho Junction, where it connects with the direct line London to Birmingham and the north, and another southwards to Newbury and Winchester.

As we leave Didcot, you will see for some miles on your right the extensive Government depôts which sprang up during the war—the Royal Army Ordnance Depôt and the Stores Depôt of the Royal Air Force. From these our soldiers and airmen on all fronts were kept supplied with equipment. Both depôts are interlaced with miles of railway track, and during the war train loads of war stores were despatched daily from here. Both are now permanent depôts of their respective services.

Next we come to Steventon and then Wantage Road Station, the latter connected by steam tram with the ancient town of Wantage, the birthplace of King Alfred. We now run through some typical Berkshire scenery—the Downs are on our left—and after Challow and Uffington Stations are passed, you see away on the Downs the famous Uffington White Horse, reported to be over a thousand years old. This "horse"—a strange looking animal—is of Saxon times, and was formed by cutting away the turf and exposing the chalk subsoil. It is believed to be the oldest of its kind, and is referred to in a charter granted to the Abbey of Abingdon between 1072 and 1084. The horse marks the site of the battle of Ashdown, fought in 871. It is said that, to commemorate the victory, King Alfred ordered his soldiers to carve the white horse—the badge or symbol of Hengist (or Stone Horse)—on the hill-side.

The next station is Shrivenham, and in a few minutes we are running into Swindon Station.

CHAPTER THE SEVENTEENTH

SWINDON

HERE we are at Swindon, and before proceeding to the Works we will pay a call at the Refreshment Rooms for lunch, and, meanwhile, have a brief chat about the town and Works.

The old town of Swindon (the town on the hill) is mentioned in Domesday Book, and it therefore dates back at least eight centuries. It was of note as an ancient market town and obtained some prosperity in the old coaching days. These census figures will shew you how the population of Swindon has increased since the establishment of the Swindon Works.

	Pop.		*Pop.*		*Pop.*		*Pop.*		*Pop.*
1831–	1,742	**1841**–	2,459	**1851**–	4,876	**1861**–	6,856	**1871**–	11,720
1881–	19,904	**1891**–	32,820	**1901**–	44,996	**1911**–	50,771	**1921**–	54,920

On December 16, 1840, the line through Swindon was opened. The building of the locomotive shops for the construction and repair of locomotives was commenced in

1841, but although the machinery was started in November of the following year, the shops were not put into general working until January 1, 1843. Brunel was mainly responsible for the planning of the Works.

You will probably be surprised to hear that from 1842 to 1895 all trains made a ten minutes stop at this station. It came about in this way: under the terms of leasing the Swindon Junction Hotel and Refreshment Rooms, the far-seeing lessees had secured an extraordinary provision that all trains should make a compulsory stop of ten minutes at Swindon for refreshments. What is more, this arrangement (if you please) was to run for ninety-nine years! In 1895, however, the Great Western Railway Company bought out the Hotel Company, the price paid being the refund of its original capital of £100,000. This was indeed a high price to pay, but it enabled much needed accelerations to be effected between London, Bath and Bristol, and to the West of England generally.

By the by, Thackeray has something to say about Swindon in those days, and also about the Great Western Railway. This extract is from his "Cockney's Travels," and alludes to a journey made some eighty-two years ago to Bristol. It was published for the first time by his daughter, Lady Ritchie, in the July 1911 issue of the *Cornhill Magazine*, of which Thackeray was the first editor:

SPECULATION IN A RAILWAY CARRIAGE: It is certain that in the midst of all the speculation, delightful as it is, ten minutes pause at Swindon, where there are twelve young women behind a counter covered with all sorts of good things which money may buy—ten minutes stop at Swindon is by no means a disagreeable interruption to those who either have eaten no dinner, or have had the good fortune to gain an appetite since that meal. The little Quakers come back munching biscuits, the red-whiskered hero wipes from his lips the froth of a pint of Dublin stout, a slight attempt at general conversation takes place, which is carried on for a while pretty briskly and audibly, because the Great Western seems to have, over other lines of road, this advantage, that one can speak without shouting, and be heard too, so excellently smooth and comfortable are the carriages and the path over which they travel.

Whilst the compulsory stop of all trains at Swindon is a thing of the past, and meals can now be taken in comfort on all the more important trains, the testimony of the great writer to the excellent running of the Great Western trains shews that, even in those early days, one of the Company's chief present-day characteristics was remarked upon.

As you will probably be aware, the main industry of Swindon is the Engine, Carriage and Wagon Building Works of the Great Western Railway Company. The Works have been very considerably extended since first constructed, and to-day they are among the largest in the world, occupying an area of 310 acres, of which 65 are roofed.

During the war immense quantities of munitions were made in the Great Western Works, including the complete manufacture of guns, shells, fuses, bombs, etc., together with parts for submarines, paravanes, howitzers, and mines. A large quantity of toluol was also produced for use in the manufacture of the T.N.T. explosive. Great Western engines, ambulance trains and wagons were a familiar sight in all fields of operations abroad. Some of the engines are still at Salonica, and some, alas! are at the bottom of the sea.

Before the war there were 663 Swindonians in the Army and Navy. Swindon's response to the Country's call in 1914 was so prompt that in two months the number had grown to 2,634. The exact number of Swindon men who served in His Majesty's forces during the Great War can never be known, but the names of 5,382 men are recorded. The Roll of Honour comprises 919 who laid down their

6 in. Guns and Travelling Carriages made at Swindon Works

lives in the struggle ; if every name were known the total would doubtless reach a thousand.

The Works are divided into three sections, viz. Locomotive, Carriage, and Wagon. It will obviously be impossible for us to make more than a hasty visit to some of the locomotive shops to-day. These are situated on the north side of the main line to Bristol and the west of England. About 7,500 men are employed in this section, which comprises Fitting, Erecting and Machine Shops, Pattern Making, Iron and Brass Foundries, also Smiths', Stamping, Coppersmiths', Boilersmiths', Tinsmiths' Shops, etc.

The extent of the Locomotive establishment will be

gathered from the fact that nearly 1,000 locomotives are repaired each year, while the capacity for constructing new locomotives is approximately two per week.

Power for the Works generally is provided by sixteen gas engines coupled direct to electric generators working at 250 volts, the total horse-power of the plant being about 4,640. The Company makes its own gas at Swindon, and, in this connection, some little time ago a new gas works on the vertical retort system was brought into use. This plant is capable of producing 3,000,000 cubic feet of gas each twenty-four hours, and is the largest privately-owned plant of its kind in the world.

In addition to the construction and repair of locomotives, carriages and wagons, a great variety of other work is done at Swindon. Large quantities of castings are made for signalling work; also the points and crossings required for the Permanent Way, etc. The repairs to pumping and hydraulic machinery in use at the various works and stations of the Company are also carried out at Swindon.

Swindon is a town of railway men, their wives and families, and it naturally takes a keen interest in matters Great Western, with which its life is so closely linked up. There is as much joy in the hearts of Swindonians over the production of a new type of locomotive as among schoolboys when an epidemic of measles gives them all an extra week's holiday!

As recently as April last, Their Majesties the King and Queen honoured Swindon Works with a visit, when they made a tour of some of the shops and saw many of the features of interest which we are going to have a look at to-day. At the conclusion of their inspection the royal saloons, drawn by engine No. 4082, "Windsor Castle," were in position for the party to entrain at the Works. Both the King and Queen were much interested in the engine, and under the guidance of the Company's Chief Locomotive Inspector, King George drove the train over

the three-quarters of a mile from the Works to Swindon Station, the first stage of the journey back to Windsor. To the delight of thousands of workpeople who assembled, Queen Mary elected to travel on the foot-plate with the King. At the conclusion of the short journey the Chief Locomotive Inspector told the King that he was an apt pupil who would soon qualify for his proficiency certificate.

And now, if you are quite ready, we will proceed direct

to the Works and see what they have to shew us there. Remember we have to be here again by 3.45 P.M., to catch the faſteſt train in the Kingdom back to London.

The Royal Party at Swindon Works, April 28th, 1924

CHAPTER THE EIGHTEENTH

"A" LOCOMOTIVE WORKSHOP

TURNING to the right on leaving Swindon Station, we find ourselves in London Street, and a short walk brings us to the entrance to the Great Western Railway Works. Before being admitted, I should like to draw your notice to the imposing building which occupies the corner site opposite. This is the G.W.R. Mechanics' Institute, which was founded in 1844 "for the purpose of disseminating useful knowledge and encouraging rational amusement amongst all classes of people employed by the Great Western Railway Company." The Institution has a fine Library of 50,000 volumes. Reading rooms, separate recreation rooms for billiards, chess and draughts, a large hall for musical and other entertainments, and a lecture hall, form part of the Institution. The

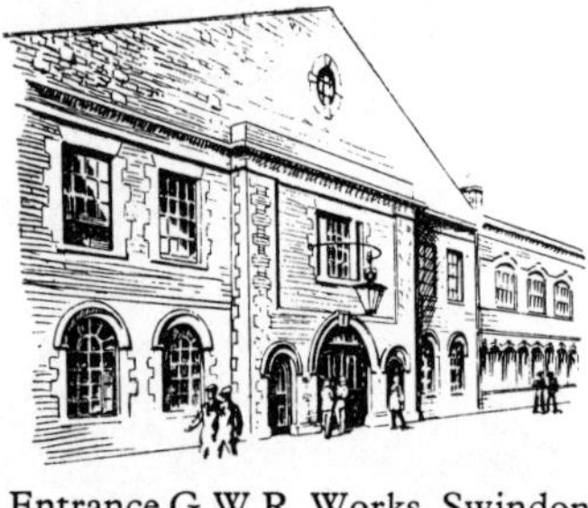

Entrance G.W.R. Works, Swindon.

management is in the hands of an elected committee of foremen and other employees. An interesting feature in connection with this Institution is that under its auspices the " annual trip," or Works' holiday, is conducted. The directors provide, free of all cost, the requisite number of trains ; and an idea of the extent of this function may be gained from the fact that this year some 29,000 employees, wives, and dependents participated. The "trip" was instituted in 1849, the number taking part on that occasion being 500.

The Works are approached by a subway from London Street; and on reaching the other end we find ourselves opposite the general offices of the Chief Mechanical Engineer. At the top of this building are situated the drawing offices.

So as to use our limited time to the best advantage we will proceed westwards alongside the line to the " A " Erecting and Machine Shop and then work back eastwards, taking some of the more interesting shops on our way.

" A " Shop, which you now see before you, ranks amongst the finest locomotive shops in the world. This shop, which has recently been considerably extended, has an area of 502,000 square feet. It really comprises several shops in one. The southern

G.W.R. Mechanics' Institute

part of the older building is appropriated to engine erectors engaged in the construction of passenger and goods engines and in repairing such engines.

Now we will pass inside and see what they have to shew us in—

"A" ERECTING SHOP

With the view of systematising the work and of minimising the occupation of the engine pits, only erecting is performed here. Such parts as frames, angle irons, cylinders, motion, etc., are prepared in the fitting shops, and handed practically ready for use to the erectors. Wonderful mechanical operations are going on all around us here.

The equipment of this shop is such that from sixty to seventy new engines can be turned out per annum, whilst the number repaired is about 600 yearly.

You see two electric traversing tables serving eighty pits. Now look overhead, there are four electric cranes having electric travelling and hydraulic lifting power. Outside the shop, on the eastern portion, there is an electric traversing table for taking engines, etc., in and out of the shop.

Here in the eastern end of the shop is installed an engine testing plant, undoubtedly one of the most ingenious examples of engineering extant. It is the only one of its kind in this country. By means of this equipment a number of valuable tests can be carried out at varying speeds, and useful data obtained as to drawbar pull, water and fuel consumption, etc.

As you see, the engine is brought in on a traverser, and the flanges of its wheels bear on grooves in the testing table. The steel rollers on which the locomotive runs are adjustable to the wheel base of any locomotive. The axles are fitted with drums, on which band brakes act for absorbing the power of the engines. As it is essential

Engine Testing Plant

that bogie and trailing wheels should be run as well as the driving wheels, all the carrying wheels of an engine under test are coupled together by means of an arrangement of belts and pulleys.

By means of this plant an engine can be run at seventy

miles an hour, at which speed the wheels are working at about 400 revolutions a minute, although the locomotive remains perfectly stationary. These tests are exceedingly instructive in demonstrating just how an engine behaves at varying speeds with all the external disturbing forces due to the road eliminated.

A power station, complete with switchboard, etc., is also situated in this portion. It comprises three vertical gas engines, developing 250 to 275 b.h.p., operating three 150-kw. generators, which provide the current for the machinery and lighting for the old and new portions of the shop.

This new portion of the shop is built on the west of the older building. It comprises engine-repairing, wheel shop, and a small section for boiler repairs, smiths' work, etc. The engine-repairing shop deals with the heavier and longer engines and rail motors, and for this purpose there are sixty pits, each 100 ft. long. The equipment for repairing is such that about 400 engines yearly, of the large type, can be dealt with.

When an engine comes in for complete overhaul, it is taken down and the parts sent to be boiled in caustic soda. When this has been done they are distributed to the various shops for any necessary work to be carried out, after which they are returned to "A" Shop for re-erecting. From the time an engine comes in till she leaves again after complete overhaul is about eight weeks. Standardisation enables a fresh—not necessarily a new—boiler to be fitted without waiting for the one taken off to be repaired.

Compressed air pipes are, as you see, fitted to the pits on one side and gas pipes on the other, obviating the pipes being carried in the columns and trailing over the ground. The plant includes six overhead electric cranes, four of

Lifting 2-8-0T Type Engine

100 tons lifting capacity each, and two of 35 tons. The 100-ton cranes have a span of 75 ft., and are fitted with two 50-ton capacity crabs, each crab having an auxiliary lift of eight tons.

We are in luck to-day, for you see they are just about to lift one of the large 2–8–0T type engines. We will time the operations. . . . There she is, lifted 5 ft. off the ground in sixty seconds exactly and travelling towards us. The travelling speed is 220 ft. a minute. These cranes are so powerful that the heaviest engine—when complete for the road—can be lifted and carried over any intervening engines to any position necessary. This special feature eliminates the necessity for any shunting with the

Traversing Tables

traverser and allows one traverser to deal with sixty pits instead of forty. There are, as you see, also traversing tables. The main table, with an engine upon it, is 42 ft. long and traverses about 520 ft. through the shop to the outside roads north and south, serving either of the sixty inside pits. It is electrically driven and equipped with an electric capstan for pulling the engines, etc., on or off the table. The engines which you see in white are in what are termed " white jackets," consisting of a covering of plastic heat non-conductor material.

" White Jackets "

Before we leave this part of the shop, take a look at this powerful hydraulic riveter which has a gap of 23 ft., and is designed for dealing with long boiler barrels of various types, also large cylindrical tanks, etc. The boilers, etc. are, as you see, handled by an overhead electric crane, which is operated from the same platform and by the same person as the hydraulic riveter.

Hydraulic Riveter

Now we will have a look at

"A" MACHINE AND FITTING SHOP

The work done in this fitting shop is the repair of parts of the modern type engines, such as motion, connecting and coupling rods, piston valves, etc., together with the preparation of new connecting and coupling rods and piston

Large Milling Machine

valves, solid and built-up cranks, etc. The built-up cranks, manufactured from purchased steel slabs and shafts, are a speciality.

A feature which you should notice here is the grinding plant. The work done on this plant is the grinding of piston rods, motion bars, quadrants and bush holes in connecting and coupling rods, etc.

These rod-milling machines deal with the coupling and connecting rods. After being forged by the steam hammer

General View of "A" Machine Shop

and then heat-treated, the ends are marked off in this shop and the bodies are milled, etc. in the machines by means of horizontal cutters, which plough a channel the length of the rod and finish the body ready for buffing. Two rods can be fluted at a time, but when the edges are done four rods can be treated simultaneously.

Here is a piece of unique equipment for fitting crossheads to piston rods. A special 50-ton press, with horizontal ram, is so arranged that the crosshead can be easily pressed on to the rod, after which the cutting of the cotter-way is finished by a broaching machine fitted for holding the crosshead and rod while the cotter-way is broached.

I thought I should have some difficulty in keeping you moving in this interesting section of the shops, but there are some wonderful things to see in the wheel shop, which is on the western side of the building.

"A" WHEEL SHOP

This section is used solely for the turning, etc., of engine and tender wheels, something like 6,000 pairs of wheels being dealt with per annum.

The operations involved in the preparation of a pair of locomotive driving wheels are many. The wheel centres are purchased as steel castings. The castings are first of all put into a large boring machine, which bores a hole in the boss for the axle. They are next marked off for the keyway, etc., then placed on a key-seating machine, which cuts the keyway. Thence they are taken to the hydraulic press, where the axle (supplied accurately machined by the machine shop) is placed in position for the wheels to be pressed on to it. Suitable keys or wedges are then fitted and driven in. The wheels (now on the axle) are next placed in a turning lathe, which turns the rims for the tyres. After this they are taken to a gas furnace, where the tyres (already bored out) are heated and shrunk on, afterwards being firmly secured by an ingenious fastening which is hammered in place by machinery. The wheels are then placed in the lathe and tyres turned on the

Wheel Lathe

tread to the correct dimensions. Next they are put in a quartering machine which bores holes to receive the crank pins.

The last operation, by no means the least important, is that of balancing, accomplished as you can see in a specially designed machine, consisting of two separate frames each carrying a bearing in which the axle journal of a pair of wheels rests. Coil springs are employed for taking the weight and thrust of the wheels and axles, and a compressed air-brake is fitted with blocks acting on the

General View of " A " Wheel Shop

front and back of each wheel. The wheels are driven by means of an electric motor with a flexible coupling as the driving member. Wheels to be tested are caused to revolve at the speed desired, and a " tachometer " is provided for indicating the speed at which they are moving, representing the maximum ordinarily reached when a locomotive is running in main line service, 60 m.p.h. Circular balance

Wheel Quartering Machine

weights are affixed to the crank-pin on each wheel proportionately to the weight computed as representing the rods to be balanced. The method of operating the machine is simple. When the wheels are revolving, spring controlled pointed rods or scribers are brought into contact with the surface at the journal bearing, which is lightly smeared with red lead, and the marks appearing on the latter, as the result of contact, indicate the point at which the wheels are out of "truth," and where alteration is necessary in the weights used for balancing. Very fine

Wheel Balancing Machine

adjustments can be made until the wheels are truly balanced. The use of this machine ensures that smooth

Duplex Hydraulic Press

running for which Great Western Railway locomotives are so famous.

This duplex hydraulic press plays an important part in the manufacture of wheels. The press, which was manufactured at Swindon, is worked at a pressure of 1,500 lb. per square inch, pressure being increased by a pump if necessary.

The gas furnace which you see in this shop is for expanding the tyres for taking off or putting on. The gas,

6-ton Electric " Goliath " Crane

with air, passes through a mixer in the correct proportions. It is then conveyed to a tubular ring, and thence through flexible tubes to the burners which surround the tyre at equal distances, thus ensuring uniform heat. To manipulate the wheels and tyres at this furnace, this 6-ton fixed electric crane is provided.

Inside the shop the wheels and axles are conveyed to and from the machines from any desired position by eleven 6-ton electrically-driven monorail cranes having a radius of 14 ft.

Now we will take a look outside at the 6-ton electric Goliath crane, which has a span of 75 ft., with a lift of 20 ft., on a track extending practically the whole length of the shop just outside the building. The crane spans five sets of double-track roads with accommodation for from 400 to 500 pairs of wheels and axles. By means of this crane any pair of wheels and axles can be lifted and conveyed as required. The travelling speed of the crane is 250 ft. per minute, traversing 100 ft. per minute and hoisting 40 ft. per minute.

6-ton Electric Monorail Crane

There are other interesting machines in the wheel shop, including a 7-ft. boring and turning mill and new model driving wheel lathes capable of taking wheels up to 86 ins. in diameter; but we must move along, for there are several other shops to visit.

You may like to know that, some twenty years ago, when alterations were being carried out and excavations being made from " A " shop to the River Ray for carrying off the storm water, the remains of a prehistoric monster, an ichthyosaurus, were discovered about 50 ft. below ground level. One portion of his fossilised bony structure was removed, but no attempt was made to recover the whole ponderous skeleton. So " Ichthy " sleeps in peace, though not intact, somewhere below where we are now standing. I do not know how many legs he had (although you can see a complete reproduction of an ichthyosaurus in the South Kensington Museum), but I think he might be classified as a 0-4-0 T (ail).

The Iron Foundry

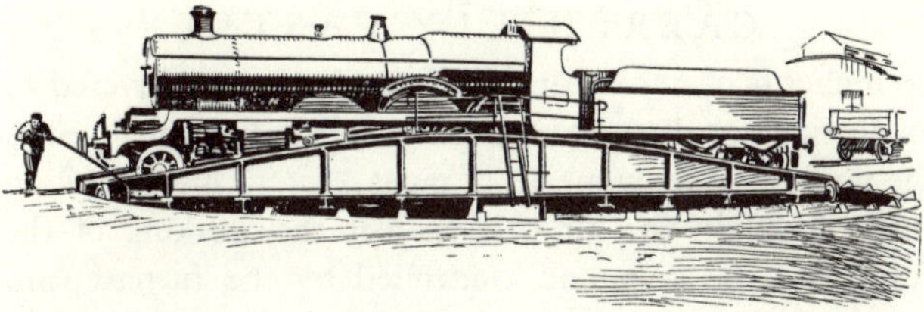

CHAPTER THE NINETEENTH

MORE LOCOMOTIVE WORKSHOPS

On leaving " A " shop we pass a 65-ft. engine turn-table, which you will be surprised to hear is so constructed and balanced that, carrying one of the largest G.W.R. locomotives and its tender, it is capable of being pushed round by one man only.

We will next visit " J " Shop. This is

THE IRON FOUNDRY

We will first go upstairs to the charging floor and see the cupolas or vertical brick-lined furnaces into which the men have been putting pig iron, scrap iron, and coke in specific proportions. The material is conveyed in a truck, which is hauled into position by hydraulic capstans, on to a 20-ton hydraulic lift, and then raised to the charging floor. We cannot remain here very long on account of the heat, as we are hardly dressed for the part.

When the furnace is filled to the level of the charging mouth, the blower producing the blast is started. Those in use here are steam driven and capable of forcing 30,000 cubic feet of air per minute against a pressure of

20 inches of water. Air from the blower is delivered to an air ring or belt surrounding the cupola and conveyed to the melting zone by means of pipes, etc. This inspection cover fitted in the air belt enables the working of the furnace to be seen and controlled by the furnaceman. Combustion of the coke in the bed melts the metal above, which trickles down and collects on the furnace bottom.

Cupolas, Iron Foundry

When sufficient metal has accumulated in the well of the furnace it is tapped through the tapping hole and passes by way of the spout into wheeled tilting ladles, being then conveyed to the moulds for casting.

Now we will go below and see the molten metal issue from the cupola at the rate of 14 to 15 tons per hour. There are five cupolas, and it is generally the practice to use two and lay up the others for repairs. The total output of finished castings is about 20,000 to 25,000 tons per annum.

One of the most interesting of the castings is the combined cylinder and saddle for a "Castle" class locomotive. For its production it is necessary to make the moulding boxes in four separate parts, together with twenty separate cores. To complete the mould these are added to each other and secured by means of large vertical cotter bolts. For the final operation the completed mould is taken to a casting pit some 6 ft. or more deep, runner boxes and risers are added, and the mould is filled with molten metal from the cupola.

Moulding Boxes for Cylinder Casting

The next point of interest on our route is "U" Shop.

THE BRASS FOUNDRY

This foundry is considered one of the best arranged in the United Kingdom. It comprises six tilting furnaces, sixteen crucible furnaces, three air furnaces—two for brass, gun-metal and phosphor bronze, and one for iron—and four moulding machines of various types, together with other appliances. The total output is in the neighbourhood of 1,700 tons per annum. The machinery for dressing and grinding, etc., is motor driven, whilst there is a dust exhausting appliance in use with the emery-grinding wheels to prevent dust being inhaled by the grinders, etc.

From the Brass Foundry we pass to "T" Shop.

THE BRASS MACHINE SHOP

In this important shop, as the name indicates, practically the whole of the brasswork for locomotive and general purposes is produced. The brass castings are supplied principally from the foundry we have just left, and include injectors, ejectors, fire appliances, water-gauges, and steam fountains. A considerable amount of work is also performed for the Engineering, Signal and Electrical Departments. Polishing of many parts of the brasswork is done by means of circular buffs, to which a device is fitted, consisting of a wrought-iron flue fixed at the back of the machine, through which the dust is drawn into a wrought-iron box by means of an electrical fan extractor. A very fine spray of water, automatically opened and closed by action of the fan, keeps the dust at the bottom of the flue. The quantity of dust so collected amounts each week to about 50 to 70 lb. You will appreciate that this arrangement must mean much for the health of the men employed here.

An interesting operation in this shop is the manufacture of pressure gauges, the testing of which by means of a hydraulic pumping machine is of great importance. The mercury is forced up glass tubes (which rise to the roof of the shop, about 33 ft. high), divided equally in pounds pressure up to 185 lb., 5 lb. pressure representing about 10 in. of mercury. By this arrangement a gauge can be adjusted to the pressure indicated by the mercury column.

The shop is fully equipped with special machinery; in fact, there are so many ingenious machines that it is difficult to single out any one for special mention, so wonderful are they all. Moreover, their operations are too intricate to admit of brief explanation. We will walk through the shop and use our eyes as much as possible.

We will now take "P2 Shop" *en route* to the Boiler Shop.

Cylinder Planer

THE CYLINDER SHOP

This shop is set apart for machining and fitting cylinders of all kinds. The approximate output is 262 pairs of cylinders per annum.

For dealing with these cylinders a special battery of boring mills, planing machines, radial drilling and

Cylinder Machining Shop

Boring Piston Valve

tapping machines is provided. This planer, which will plane a surface 8 ft. long by 6 ft. wide and 6 ft. high, has an attachment for planing to the proper radius the portion of the cylinder which fits the smoke-box saddle. This is only one of a large number of interesting machines which we can watch at work as we walk through to

THE BOILER SHOP

This really comprises four different shops, but we can only visit the largest, which is " V " shop.

Here, again, you must use your eyes as much as possible, for I am afraid the noise of a boiler shop is hardly conducive to carrying on an easy conversation.

Boiler work has always been in the front rank at Swindon, and it is not too much to say that the workmanship in this shop is second to none. In later years machinery has figured very largely in boiler construction, and if you will look around you will see that the Swindon Boiler Shop is thoroughly and efficiently equipped in this direction. Take a look at this large combined slotting and drilling machine, of which you saw a photograph in the train. The four heads work simultaneously on the bed, and will slot up to eight $1\frac{1}{4}$ in. engine frames, laid one on the other.

Among numerous interesting appliances perhaps one specially worthy of notice is this large hydraulic flanging press. It works at a pressure of 750 pounds to the square inch, and consists principally of three main rams, which operate in cylinders fixed in the ground, giving the table on which the plates, etc., are placed an upward movement.

Drilling Bay, Boiler Shop

Large Bending Rolls

Adequate means for expeditiously handling various heavy plates in this and other presses are provided by cranes, which are of Swindon make, one having a capacity of five, and the other of three, tons. The equipment of the press plant is completed by two furnaces for heating the plates.

Hydraulic Flanging Press

A special feature of the boiler shop work is the flanging of cold copper plates in the big press. The operations are carried out by means of cast-iron blocks (an inside block and an outside die), machined to the required shape and dimensions, between which the plates are pressed. You will be interested to know that this shop was the first to introduce this system, which has since become practically universal.

Besides the cranes mentioned, the shop is equipped with upwards of thirty jib cranes from 20 cwt. to 30 cwt. capacity, which greatly facilitate the handling of the heavy plates, and which happily are the means of reducing personal injuries to a minimum.

A large amount of rolling is performed here, and there are three sets of rolls for bending and one for levelling. The weight of the big roll is over twenty tons.

As your ears have already appreciated, riveting is an essential feature of boiler work. This noise results from the use of portable pneumatic riveters, for the three large hydraulic riveting machines which we see at work are silent in operation. The largest of these has a crane working in conjunction with it capable of lifting 30 tons. As you see, it lifts the boiler and casing, etc., when bolted together, and suspends them whilst the riveter presses the rivet into shape. The force exerted is equal to 45 tons on the rivet.

A part of this shop is set aside for the manufacture of copper stays, the equipment consisting of saws, centring rolls and lathes for turning and screwing. The weekly output in this section averages about 12,000 stays.

The general excellence and equipment of the shop ensures G.W.R. boilers being built in a systematic manner. It also permits of their being expeditiously passed to the Tube department, where the tubes are put in and expanded and beaded by up-to-date pneumatic machinery. Thence they are handed to the boiler mounters for the fitting of regulators, water-gauges, superheaters, etc., after which they are passed to the steam and hydraulic testing shed to ensure that all joints and parts are steam-tight. The boilers are painted and are then ready for the engine frames. We now come to

THE ROLLING MILLS

These mills were originally used for working up old rails and re-rolling them into new, but with the introduction of steel rails they were adapted for the production of bars, etc. The mills are really made up of

" Pile" in Cogging Mill

four independent mills, known as " cogging or blooming," " finishing," " medium," and " guide " mills.

We have not time to do more than just take a look at one or two of the mills at work, but perhaps I ought to explain that scrap iron received from the various departments is sorted into grades for manufacturing purposes. It is then taken to the shears, where it is cut

into the desired lengths, cleaned, and scaled in a drum preparatory to being put into a " pile," which is cubical in shape and weighs about 2½ cwt. The pile is conveyed to a welding furnace, where it is heated for about two hours and then taken to the steam hammer, the number of blows required to give the desired shape being from 100 to about 150. These pieces of iron are again heated in a welding furnace, the heat of which is raised to 2,700° F., the heating period being from one to two hours. They are then taken out and conveyed to the rolls for shaping. The piles are about 9 in. to 10 in. square by 3 ft. long. They are now placed in the furnace, where they remain another two hours, and on being withdrawn are taken to the cogging mill to be reduced to the desired shapes for the finishing mill. Here they are rolled to the required sections, cut to lengths by a saw or shears, inspected, and loaded into trucks.

There are twelve furnaces, ten welding and two puddling. The latter are used for " balling " together the turnings from the various shops, and then taken to the steam hammer, afterwards going through the same process as the iron and steel piles. About 200 tons of sections and finished bars of various kinds are turned out weekly for the various departments. Steam is generated in the boilers situated on top of the furnace by the waste heat from the furnaces to supply the engines

driving the hammers and mills. You may be interested to know that the quantity of coal required to heat a ton of iron is about 8 cwt.

This section and the steam

hammers should be seen at night, when the glowing white-hot metal and showers of sparks which fly from it under the hammers constitute a firework display of no mean order.

Our next call is at "K" shop.

COPPERSMITHS' SHOP

The various items of interest here are far too numerous to refer to individually. The work carried

Coppersmiths' Shop

on is copper and tin smithing in connection with engines and tenders.

A description of the manufacture of one of the shop

products, that well-known adornment of a locomotive boiler, the brass safety valve cover, may interest you. The flat sheet is obtained from the stores and cut to the desired shape from a pattern furnished by the coppersmith. The bottom portion is dealt with first, the edges to be brought together and brazed being filed to a feather edge and cut to form "cramps," which, when closed up by hand, make the joint, this in turn being brazed, thus forming a tapered barrel. The top portion is also bent by hand, and after the same operations forms a parallel barrel. Each portion is then beaten out by hand and by a pneumatic hammer to the desired shape, smoothed by a boxwood mallet on a steel-headed tool, blackleaded to shew the hammer marks plainly, and hammered or planished with a bright-faced hammer. Afterwards the top edge of the top portion is wired, forming a bead and at the same time strengthening the cover. The bottom edge of the bottom portion is beaded only. After these operations the two portions are brazed together and the

Pneumatic Hammer

seam of the joint filed and smoothed by hammer, the cover then being ready for the polishing lathe and afterwards for fixing to the engine.

Another special feature in copper-smithing is the making of joints on pipe ends, the latest method being to press the end of the pipe in the form of a collar or cone. This is done in a hydraulic press, making a much safer joint than under the old style, in which brazing figured. The method of bending pipes will interest you. First of all the pipe is softened or annealed, then filled with resin so that in bending it may retain its circular shape, and afterwards bent by machine or by hand. The pipe-bending machine in this shop is capable of dealing with most difficult shapes; in fact, from two to twelve bends can be accomplished by means of it in one pipe.

The pneumatic hammer which you see here is very simple in construction, and will give any number of blows up to 300 per minute.

Tinsmiths and lamp-makers are also part of the staff of the shop and make all sorts of tin articles, such as lamps, cans, machinery guards, etc.

Now we enter, I think you will agree, one of the most fascinating shops in the Works—

"R" MACHINE SHOP

It is regarded as one of the show shops of the Works on account of its up-to-date mechanical equipment, which includes wonderful labour and time-saving appliances of extremely ingenious design. Watch them closely. You see they are carrying out their intricate operations without any human assistance beyond being fed from time to time with bars of steel.

The general work of the shop consists of the repair and renewal of the locomotive valve gear, motion, etc.,

" R " Machine Shop

together with an enormous amount of repetition work such as the production of stay-bolts for boilers.

Take a good look at this patent automatic turret lathe. There are fourteen of these machines in use, and they are principally employed on the production of vertical stays for Belpaire, etc., boilers, bolts, pins of all descriptions, and stays for fire-boxes. The operations of producing, say, a vertical stay, are three, viz. the middle of the bar is first turned out, then both ends are simultaneously screwed, and, lastly, the stay is parted off. All the operations and changes from one process to another are entirely automatic. This is the essence of the automatic system, and greatly reduces the cost of producing these important items of boiler work.

We cannot spend over much time here, and any attempt to describe the varied and extensive operations carried out in this shop would occupy the whole of our time, I fear.

Here is another automatic machine turning out engine hand-rail knobs threaded complete, which, like the stay rods, are delivered perfectly finished into containers which, you see, are being collected periodically by means of an electric truck.

I anticipated a little difficulty in getting you away from this shop, but there are some other interesting places to visit, and we must get along to the

STAMPING SHOP

Here is a shop which is indeed a *striking* example of modern methods. In it, by means of drop stamps or hammers, are produced the smaller forgings required for engines, tenders, etc. The different articles manufactured here are of wide variety, and number about four hundred. As you will see, the drop stamp consists mainly of a steam cylinder, fixed overhead, and two uprights between which the tup, or hammer, works on to the hammer block. The principal features of drop stamping are the die blocks top and bottom. For each type of forging die blocks have to be made, and, briefly stated, the forging is produced by the tup or hammer, on to which is usually fixed the top die block, forcing the heated metal on to the bottom die block, which is fixed to the hammer block. The special features of drop

Battery of Steam Stamps

stamping are rapidity of production and cleanness of the forgings, the latter being so marked as practically to obviate any subsequent machining.

We will walk through

THE SMITHS' SHOP

which, you will see, is used for general smithing and contains about thirty fires.

In all large works, I suppose, pranks are not entirely unknown, and I heard (quite unofficially, of course), during a recent visit to Swindon, of the newcomer who was sent from the Smiths' Shop to Stores for a bucket of blast when the fan to the fire was not working properly.

Smiths' Shop

Others despatched for "sky hooks," when shafting is being erected, are like the new boys at school who are sent to the stationers' for a map of the "Undiscovered Islands." Boys never *really* grow up !

The Smiths' Shop leads us to

THE BOLT SHOP

Here is a machine specially worthy of notice. It is a 2 in. nut-making machine. You see that the piercing

Nut-making Machine

Steam Hammer Forge

punches, etc., of this machine are worked independently of each other. A heated bar is pushed by the operator (who stands in front of the machine) against adjustable stocks, and the nut is made complete by dies and punches. The machine is capable of making five or six large nuts at one heat of bar, and ten or twelve small sized nuts. It runs continuously, but is so fed that the operator has no difficulty in feeding the bar forward each time. The punches are kept cool by a constant stream of water running over them, for which pipes and cocks are fitted.

Next we will shew you something which I think will be of outstanding interest—

THE STEAM HAMMERS

These are now used for the manufacture of large forgings, such as connecting rods, valve rods, quadrants, and extension frames, the last varying from 2 in. to 4 in. in thickness, and being from 12 in. to 2 ft. wide and about 10 ft. 3 in. long. In addition, general forgings up to about 2 tons are made up from scrap iron. This forge is equipped with eight steam hammers ranging from 15 cwt. to 5 tons. Steam for the hammers is obtained from boilers fixed over the top of the furnaces. The hammers are under perfect control, and will crack a nut without injury to the kernel. If you will place your watch under the hammer, the operator will demonstrate the nicety with which it can be used. . . .

There you are—the 5 ton steam hammer has not pounded your watch to pieces, but you could hardly place a piece of tissue paper between the hammer and your watch glass. Yet the crushing effect of that hammer upon a piece of hot iron is as great as that produced by a load of 30 tons! Yes, you get your watch back all right in this trick.

I see it has now turned three o'clock. We will, therefore, conclude our tour with a visit to

THE TESTING HOUSE

It may be divided into two main sections—one dealing with the testing of general material and the other for

Testing House

testing chains and other lifting appliances. We are more concerned with the former to-day, for in this section and in this 60-ton hydraulic machine are tested all steel and copper boiler plates. About 150 to 200 are dealt with weekly. The machine is also used for crushing, hardness and transverse tests. Special steels are tested by means of an extensometer, which registers the elongation, and is so sensitive as to be able to record an elongation of 0·001 of an inch.

A sample of copper plate, 8 in. in length, is now being placed in the hydraulic testing machine, and we will watch the process. You see as more pressure is exerted the indicator gradually moves along until it registers 12 tons—and then—CRACK—the piece of metal has broken. Now, measuring it after test, we find that it is 11 in. in length, so that it has stretched some 3½ in. before parting.

There are many other interesting testing machines in this section : a chain testing machine, capable of exerting a pull of 100 tons, used for testing chains, wire, and other ropes, etc. ; a hardness testing machine, which operates by ball indentation ; and an impact machine, which tests steel under shock, among others.

We must, however, leave these machines, and also, I fear, a number of shops, unvisited if we are to have our trip back to London by the famous 3.45 p.m. train, and make our way from Swindon Works to Swindon Station. Although we have not been able to visit the whole of the locomotive shops we have certainly seen some of the more interesting of them, and, I think, we have acquired a good general idea of locomotive construction.

As we pass stationwards, we see in the yard two powerful travelling cranes. These cranes are capable of lifting the largest and heaviest locomotives on the Great Western Railway.

The whole of the shops we have seen, and those we have not seen, constitute a vast machine fed with iron, steel, copper, and other materials, which are passed through

various sections of the machinery and ultimately emerge as Great Western Railway locomotives. Surely, this is modern magic and more fascinating than any conjuring trick.

And now we are going to see one of these wonderful locomotives in actual operation, hauling the fastest train in the Kingdom.

CHAPTER THE TWENTIETH

THE FASTEST TRAIN

Now I have got a pleasant surprise for you. We are not only going to travel to London by the fastest train, but *on the foot-plate* of the engine of the fastest train. I am sure you will welcome and enjoy such an experience, which hardly comes the way of every schoolboy.

Here comes the famous train, which is the 2.30 P.M. from Cheltenham, having called at Gloucester and Stroud *en route*. She is due here at 3.40 P.M., away at 3.45 P.M., and timed to arrive at Paddington at 5.0 P.M., covering the $77\frac{1}{4}$ miles in 75 minutes, which averages about 62 miles an hour. Incidentally I may add, and you will bear me out when our trip is over, there is no finer stretch of permanent way in the world than that between Swindon and Paddington.

You see the engine of our train is No. 4082 "Windsor Castle," the identical engine driven by His Majesty King George. Our foot-plate trip is to be on one of the latest and most powerful locomotives.

Now let us step on to the foot-plate and pay our

respects to Messrs. Driver and Fireman. You notice at once what a roomy cab the engine has. If we stand over here we shall not be in the way and we can see all that is going on. If so inclined, or if you are tired of standing, you can occupy one of the tip-up seats which are a feature of Great Western Railway locomotives.

Take a look at the steam pressure gauge and vacuum gauges. You see the needle of the former indicates a boiler pressure of 220 lb. per square inch, and the vacuum gauge needles record a "nil" vacuum in the train pipe and about 22 in. of vacuum in the reservoir, indicating that the brakes are fully applied.

You will also observe that the fire-hole doors are open, but the flap plate is up in position, the dampers are closed, and the right-hand injector is working. These conditions are necessary in order to prevent the blowing off of steam while the engine is standing at the platform, for the "body" of the fire is considerable.

Notice that the reversing screw is in the "full fore" gear, or what the driver would call 75 per cent. cut off position. It is nearly time for us to be off on our record run. The water level is at the top of the gauge glass, and the fireman is now opening the rear dampers. The driver opens the steam valve of the ejector and releases the brakes. Watch the vacuum gauge. You see the needle rises gradually till it registers a vacuum of 25 inches.

As it is fine to-day the rails are quite dry, but had they been wet and greasy they would be well sanded by means

of the sanding gear so that the wheels could get a good grip on the rails. If the engine had been standing any considerable time, the cylinder cocks would also be opened, in order to blow out any water resulting from condensation in the cylinders.

There goes the guard's whistle. If you look out towards the rear of the train, you will see he is giving us the " Right away " by waving his green flag. Our driver acknowledges this by a blast on the engine whistle. Now I want you to watch the driver's operations closely. You see he is gradually opening the regulator valve by pulling over the regulator handle to about one-eighth of its full opening. He pauses, and the engine starts ever so gradually. He now moves the regulator to about half or three-quarters open position, and, as you see, our speed increases and we are off on our non-stop run to London.

As our engine accelerates, the driver varies the position of the gear, and, from what you have already been told, you know that the reason for this is to diminish the period of steam admission at each stroke of the engine until at high speed the " cut-off " position is about 17 per cent. of the stroke. Should any further reduction in power be necessary the driver will slightly close the regulator. As you see, we are now running in 17 per cent. cut off and at half regulator.

In the meantime, the steam valve of the ejector has been closed, the vacuum being maintained while running by the air-pump actuated direct by a crosshead. The feed of the lubricator has also been readjusted. Had the cylinder cocks been open at starting, they would now have been closed.

You noticed, I think, that the fireman stirred up his fire as soon as we got away from the station, and now he is busy throwing shovelfuls of coal upon it. Observe how he breaks up any large lumps, and also how he keeps the coal well watered, and also the foot-plate, to lay the dust. He obtains his water from a pipe attached to a convenient control cock on the cab side.

The fireman has now shut off the right-hand injector and started the left-hand, or exhaust steam, injector. The latter is generally worked for the greater part of the trip, the rate of feed being about equal to the demands of the boiler. This injector is often only shut off when the regulator is closed, no exhaust steam then being available, in which case the right-hand, or live steam, injector would, if necessary, be used. The fireman operates the injectors to suit the rise and fall of the steam pressure, fluctuations of the water level, and the working conditions prevailing, with due regard, of course, to those to be encountered.

As we sight Marston Crossing signal box, our whistle is blown to give warning of approach. You will notice that this is done at all crossings, junctions, and at principal stations.

Now we are indeed well under way, and will time our running. I will start my watch at the next quarter mile post, and stop it at the following one. You see the watch indicates the speed on the dial. . . . We have taken exactly 15 seconds to run over the section 72 to 71 : 111 (i.e. 72 miles to $71\frac{3}{4}$ miles from Paddington), so our speed here—Shrivenham—is exactly 60 miles per hour.

As you see, the driver's attention is on the road ahead, where he is noting the position of the up main line signals, all of which have been "off," signifying that we may proceed. Should we approach any "distant" signal in the "Danger" position, he would immediately check speed and be prepared to stop dead at the next "home" signal, should this also be at "Danger."

Whistling as we approach, we pass Ashbury, and then Knighton Crossings, and now we are through Uffington, and note our speed has increased to 67 miles per hour. The air is much clearer than it was this morning, and your friend the "White Horse" stands out clearly in the afternoon sun. Now we pass Challow, and then Wantage Road, at 74 miles per hour, reaching Steventon Station at 4.5½ P.M., our correct scheduled passing time. Running by the R.A.F. and R.A.O.D. Depôts, we pass Didcot at 4.9 P.M. We speed onwards through Cholsey and Moulsford. Now you see a train approaching us on the Down line. In a flash she is past and gone on her way westwards. This is the 3.15 P.M. train from Paddington to Gloucester. We cross the Thames and run through Goring and Streatley Station.

Here, you see, the fireman crosses over to the right-hand side of the tender, unfastens the water pick-up scoop control, and lowers the scoop by turning the handle as we approach the Goring troughs. Now keep your eye on the water indicator, and you will see how rapidly the tank is filling. You notice that the fireman commences to raise the scoop by turning the handle just before the tank is full. This is in order to avoid overfilling. We have picked up 1,500 gallons of water in 11 seconds, without making any "splash" about it.

We now pass Pangbourne and run alongside the Thames at Tilehurst. Soon we are approaching Reading, and at West Junction we see the engine sheds and turn-table on our right. We run through Reading Station at 4.25 P.M. Our speed varies but little as we

Water Troughs, Goring

meet the 3.55 P.M. train Paddington to South Wales and pass through Sonning Cutting, Twyford, Maidenhead, Taplow, and on to Slough, which we reach at 4.39 P.M., 1½ minutes in front of our scheduled passing time. We are through Langley at 4.40½ P.M.

Take a look at the water-gauge, and you will see that the level is one inch down in the glass. The fireman will allow it to drop from now onwards to the end of the trip, by less frequent use of his injectors. You will also notice that he has eased up with his firing, and he will add no more coal to the furnace. We are through West Drayton Station at 4.41½, pass the 4.30 P.M. train Paddington to Plymouth and then Hayes and Harlington Station at 4.46. The fireman revives his fire with the pricker, and then assists the driver in looking out for signals, etc. The former's more strenuous duties have finished for this trip.

At 4.48 we pass Southall Station, then run over the Wharncliffe Viaduct and through Hanwell, West Ealing and Ealing Broadway Stations. Here we note that the distant signals are painted a distinctive yellow with a black stripe. This colour scheme for distant signals continues into Paddington, and the lenses of the signal lamps are of a similar colour.

On we speed through Acton, passing the Old Oak Common engine and carriage sheds. The driver shuts down the regulator, eases the handle back into the drifting or coasting position to ensure lubrication of the cylinders, and places the gear in the 45 per cent. position.

Now he tests the brakes by slightly opening the air valve of the ejector, causing a gradual momentary application, which you see is indicated by the movement of the train pipe vacuum gauge needle, and by slight reduction in speed. Satisfied with the response he obtains, he immediately releases the brake by closing the air valve and opening the steam valve, until the train pipe vacuum is again 25 inches.

With a gradually decreasing speed, the driver's hand on the air valve in case of emergency or signal check, we drift on through Westbourne Park and Royal Oak Stations into Paddington Station. A gradual application of the brakes brings us to rest at No. 8 platform at 4.58 P.M., or just two minutes in front of our scheduled time. More than splendid, or I am prepared to adopt your schoolboy parlance, and vote it a " corking " run !

You noticed, I think, that the driver opened the steam valve and closed the air valve just before we stopped. This was to ensure that the brake was only just, if at all, applied at the moment of actually stopping. He did this in order to avoid stopping with even any suspicion of a jerk.

You see the fire is now quite low and the water level only one inch above the bottom of the gauge glass. The pressure is about 200 lb. per square inch and gradually falling, for the right-hand injector is again at work filling the boiler to prevent it blowing off in the station. Now we will thank Messrs. Driver and Fireman for a splendid run of 77¼ miles in 73 minutes, and bid them Good-bye !

Well, I trust you have spent an enjoyable and instructive time. What you were told yesterday and what you have seen to-day at Swindon Works, crowned by your experience of a 77 miles non-stop run on the footplate of the fastest train in the Kingdom, should, as our American friends say, " put you wise " concerning the construction and operation of a railway locomotive.

You will now be able to enlighten your school-fellows on a point or two, and it is within the realms of possibility that you may be able to tell some of your elders a few things about the railway engine that *even they* do not know.

You have seen how first-class workmanship and mechanical skill and ingenuity are blended in each operation connected with the construction of a G.W.R. locomotive so as to ensure that speed, smoothness of running, and reliability for which Great Western Railway trains are world-famous, and which have helped to make the initials " G.W.R. " the indelible hall-mark of railway efficiency.

Now I know boys just hate " moral " stories. I mean stories with a " goody-goody " moral tacked on to them. Well, the moral to our story is not " goody-goody," but it is certainly good. You have heard it before. It is, in fact, a little three-word slogan, which I commend to you and all your friends, for it is to everyone's advantage to keep it in mind in connection with business and pleasure travel. It is at once an invitation, a piece of excellent advice, and (if you will) a polite command. Untold thousands of business folk and pleasure seekers have adopted it with thankfulness, and very sensibly passed on to others. It is, of course,

" GO GREAT WESTERN."

You can bear me out that "the going's good."

AU REVOIR